ASIAN GIRL IN A SOUTHERN WORLD

DALENA H. BENAVENTE

ISBN: 978-0-9983873-0-7

DEDICATION

*To everyone with an untold story,
and to all of those who have felt alone. To those who
don't wear their pain on their face for attention. To
those who do not give in to the victim mentality. To
those who do not allow themselves to be manipulated
by the selfish ones. To those who are brave enough to
be impervious to being guilt-tripped. To those who
swallow tears but give them permission to exist. To
everyone with an overcomer's spirit. To those who have
made it their purpose to be victorious. To those who
cook because it helps them deal with life. I acknowledge
you. We are few and growing smaller, unless we do
something about it. Choose to do something about it.
This is my something. This is to you.
This is for us.*

A story so unique you have to eat it

to believe it

TABLE OF CONTENTS

INTRODUCTION

Desire. That's why I'm writing this book. I have a deep desire to transport readers to a place in Tennessee that is so remote and historically unimportant that the chances are, unless you've lived there, you've probably never heard of it and probably never will, save for this book. Why do I want to take you there? Because there is a story that took place there that I think you will either relate to, or find very interesting, and that story is my life. I grew up in the 1980's- not a good era for brown skin and black hair- even worse if you grew up in the racially charged, Confederate-flag-flying, rarely-on-any-map part of the world where I'm from. It's a place where, when kids grow up, they live down the road from their parents who have always lived down the road from theirs. It's a place where you can find six generations in a single row at the cemetery, and people know where you'll be buried the day that you are born. It's a place where, despite the immensely sheltered lifestyle and lack of tolerance for diversity, I still say to this day that the best people I've ever had the pleasure of knowing are from. That's why this has to be a recipe book. It's not enough to tell the stories. You can't just read about it, hear about it or imagine it. You can't, because it's just too much. In order to truly understand these stories that I have to tell, you have to eat them. You have to put them in your mouth, taste them, swallow them, and know they are real. My hope is that you'll read a story from here and make the corresponding recipe. I hope my noodles make you laugh, my cake makes you want to hug someone you love, and I hope my sangria makes you want to fight for what you believe in. This is my story. This is *Asian Girl in a Southern World*.

KITCHEN THEOLOGY

Preparing to Cook:

Before making any new recipe, take basic steps to put yourself in the best frame of mind possible to ensure the highest quality result. If applicable, hair should be pulled back away from the face and shoulders, hands clean, counters and stove wiped down. Do yourself a favor by laying out all of the ingredients for the recipe, along with the clean tools and dishes required. Freshly sharpened knives will give you confidence should you need to do any cutting. Keep kitchen scissors handy to help with the opening of any plastic packaging of newly purchased ingredients. Having a dishtowel nearby for wiping your hands or small spills is also very helpful. Have your recipe in printed form close by for reference, along with a pen or pencil to record helpful notes, should you decide to make it again later. And yes, feel free to write notes in the cookbook itself. After all, it's yours anyway.

Kitchen Notes:

Bologna: Pronounced "buh-low-nee." It's basically hot dog contents in a different shape with slightly different seasonings- definitely not a choice meat for a health nut or carnivore connoisseur. It is, however, a protein that is commonly used and even celebrated in the part of the south where I'm from. Most people purchase it pre-sliced in packages, but if you have the option of asking someone behind a deli counter to slice it thick for sandwiches, well, put on your fancy pants and do that instead.

Cast Iron: Yes. Always yes. Use it whenever you can. Cast iron retains heat so if you serve your meal directly from the pan, it will stay warmer longer. There are also no strange chemical ingredients in cast iron like some coated pans. Cooking with cast iron will also benefit your dinner guests who are anemic. The more you use it, the easier it becomes to clean and even grows in value over time. Yes to cast iron. Always yes.

Coconut Milk: Be very clear, there are TWO kinds: the kind you drink, and the kind you cook with. The kind you *drink* is found in the refrigerated milk section of the grocery store or on the shelf in a cardboard container. The kind you *cook with* is also found on a shelf, usually in the international section, in a standard sized can.

Fish Sauce: Fish sauce is made by packing fresh caught anchovies in salt and letting them ferment for up to twelve months. The salt breaks down the flesh of the fish. The liquid that is left after straining is the fish sauce. Doesn't that sound delicious? Of course not, but it is a prized staple ingredient in many Asian dishes. It's very stinky and very salty. If you are going to use it, use it sparingly. Of course if you get a whiff of it and decide that it's just not for you, it's okay. Don't let it discourage you from cooking Asian food altogether. However, should the time come that you need some real street cred when it comes to your Asian cooking, nonchalantly bring up that you use fish sauce. They'll think you're the real deal.

Mixers: Fancy stand-up or handheld electric? That is the question. My answer? Either. Or both. You do what's best for you whenever you're cooking. Problem solved.

Moonshine: Moonshine is a clear liquor made of corn mash, sugar, yeast and water that can measure up to 200 proof, and has been distilled by moonlight in backwoods Tennessee since the 1800s. My experience with moonshine is that it was always very available and very illegal. Tennessee's liquor laws loosened in 2009, which lead to the first legal distillery (Ole Smoky Distillery) opening its doors in 2010. It has a strong fumy sensation, comes in a variety of flavors, and tastes like it can power your lawn mower if you are out of gas.

Muscadine Wine: Muscadines are a variety of grape that is native to the Southeastern United States. They don't grow in bunches like typical grapes do, and the muscadines are larger in size. The skin is thicker and pulls away from the pulp more easily. They are just delicious when ripened on the vine, so southerners started doing the next logical thing- making wine with them.

Produce: I feel like this is common sense, but for any new cooks out there who have not had a mentor for basic cooking knowledge, use fresh fruits and vegetables that are in season and haven't been picked until ripened on the vine or tree. It's becoming harder and harder to find this type of produce. Just ask anyone who has ever eaten a *real* tomato. Seek out local farmer's markets and create trade agreements with your neighbors who have gardens. Everything from your salads to fruit pies will thank you.

Soy Sauce Storage: Soy sauce is best kept in a cool dark place. Storing it in light or heat will cause it to lose it freshness. If no such place is available, it should be refrigerated.

Washing Rice: This is a big debate in the rice cooking world. I'm from the "wash your rice" camp. I prefer doing this because it rids the rice of stray pebbles and unnecessary starches, which can cause the rice to be clumpy and can muddle the flavor. If you want to eat clean rice that isn't super sticky, then wash your rice. If you want to eat rice that is creamy, starchy (and possibly dirty), don't wash it. Rice is a grain. Grains come from plants. Plants grow in dirt. That means some dirt, leaves and pebbles will be involved. That's why I wash my rice. Here's how I do it: after I measure my rice, I take it to the sink and run cool water over it until it's an inch above the top of the rice. I swirl it around seven or eight times. Some Asian elders believe that you should never change the direction of the swirling because there's a risk that you could break the grains. I've never noticed any harm with the particular brands that I use. The water will appear milky. I pour out the water and repeat the process two more times.

Favorite Ingredient Brands:

(These can be purchased online if they are not found in your grocery store)

Rice:

Botan Calrose (California, USA)

Hinode Calrose (Himalayan Foothills, India)

Roland Jasmine (Thailand)

Soy Sauce:

Kikkoman Lite (Japan)

Coconut Milk:

canned: Chaoko (Thailand)

drinkable: Califia Farms (San Joaquin Valley, CA)

Moonshine:

Full Throttle Sloonshine (Trimble, TN)

Ole Smoky (Gatlinburg, TN)

Whiskey:

Knob Creek (Clermont, KY)

Bourbon:

Knob Creek (Clermont, KY)

Muscadine Wine:

Duplin Winery (Rose Hill, North Carolina)

Childress Vineyards (Lexington, North Carolina)

Smoked Chocolate Chips:

Hot Cakes (Seattle, Washington)

Fish Sauce:

Red Boat (Phú Quốc, Vietnam)

ASIAN GIRL IN A SOUTHERN WORLD

Some names and identifying details have been changed to protect the privacy of individuals.

CHAPTER ONE

NOT LIKE THE OTHERS

One of the these things is not like the others.

There are many of them, but she is one.

The one with black hair.

The one with brown skin.

The one with fire in her eyes.

She's made darker by the white walls,

white floor and white blankets.

She's made darker by the silence in her cry.

She is the thing that is not like the others.

And so she was destined.

And so she will always be.

WHITE TOWN

I was born in a white town, in a white county, in a mostly white state. Where I'm from many people still use the word "n" word regularly, and it rolls off their tongues as naturally as if it were a word as common as "water." You can find the Confederate flag flying high in cemeteries and proudly displayed in the back windows of oversized trucks, as a decorative backdrop to the driver's gun rack. It's common to hear a KKK reference every couple of months. There are very few black people, and Asians...what are those?

I was born on July 18, 1977 in Union City, Tennessee. I share a birthday with Nelson Mandela. I've wondered if we sounded the same when we cried our first cries. Most of the nurses in the hospital had never seen an Asian baby before, so when I arrived, even the nurses who weren't working in the maternity ward came to see what I looked like. I wasn't hard to miss among the rows and rows of newborn babies. I was "the brown baby with the jet black hair." My father is a white American and my mother is a first-generation immigrant from the Philippines, so I'm technically half-white and half-Filipino. It made no difference. When you live in the trailer park in Woodland Mills (population

526), half-Filipino meant I wasn't white. At the time of my birth, the Asian population in town included two people: my mom and me. We lived three hours west of Nashville, two hours north of Memphis, twenty minutes from the Mississippi River, and right in the middle of nowhere. My dad worked the graveyard shift at the Goodyear Tire and Rubber Factory and took as much overtime as he could get. It was hard labor. *Real* hard. He cooked tires which caused him to come home coughing up black matter. It was the same job as many people who lived in the thirty-mile radius, and it was considered good and respectable work. My mom stayed home. She said the local people with their southern drawls had a hard time understanding what she was saying due to her thick Filipino accent. As a result, she didn't like to leave the trailer much. My mom will tell anyone to this day that the reason she wanted a baby was because she was lonely and bored, and wanted someone to be with while Dad was at work, so that's how and why I came to be in this world. I was the Asian baby who lived in a trailer in the remote Tennessee woods, born on Nelson Mandela's birthday. The trailer in the woods was all I knew for years. To me, it was my whole world. It was my whole Southern world.

Spicy Brown Sugar Meatballs in Average White Sauce

YIELD: 6-8 servings

MEATBALLS:

- 2-2.5 lbs. ground beef
- 2 eggs, beaten
- 1 cup Italian Bread Crumbs
- 1 Tbs. brown sugar
- 2 tsp. red pepper flakes
- 3 cloves minced garlic
- 1 tsp. salt
- 1 tsp. ground pepper
- ½ tsp. grated nutmeg

GLAZE:

- ½ cup brown sugar, packed
- 2 Tbs. balsamic vinegar
- 3 Tbs. water
- 1 Tbs. milk

Preheat oven to 350 degrees. Cover a 13 x 18" sheet pan with foil and spray with nonstick spray. Place all meatball ingredients in a bowl and mix thoroughly with your hands. Shape into 1 ½" balls and place on prepared pan. Bake for 8 minutes, then rotate the meatballs and cook for another 10. While meatballs bake, place all glaze ingredients in large saucepan and stir over medium-high heat until combined and starting to thicken. Take the meatballs out of the oven and place directly into the saucepan. Stir so that the meatballs are completely covered with glaze.

AVERAGE WHITE SAUCE:

- 4 Tbs. butter or bacon fat
- 4 Tbs. all-purpose flour
- 2½ cups milk, heated on low just until bubbles form
- Nutmeg, about 8-10 grates fresh or a dash of dry (or to taste)
- Salt and pepper to taste

Melt the butter over medium low heat. Stir in the flour making a paste, and cook for 2 minutes, taking care to make sure it doesn't brown. Stir in the hot milk. The sauce will thicken. Bring to a gentle boil. Add in nutmeg, salt, and pepper to taste. Stir for another minute and remove from heat.

ASSEMBLY & EATING:

This is a recipe, so I'm supposed to tell you what these meatballs look like on a plate. I'm not. I'm supposed to tell you what to serve with it on the side. I won't. I'm going to tell you that if you want to eat these meatballs in the very best way, you'll need a small group of people you know, or a small group of people that you want to break the ice with pretty quickly. You will all need to stand over your stove with two things: a trash can placed across the room, and a shot glass full of toothpicks. Stab a meatball with a toothpick and drag it through the white sauce- yes, in the pans that you cooked them in. Eat it. Close your eyes and chew slowly. After you swallow, toss your toothpick into the trash can. It's fun, so do it again. That's right, eat another one. Now this time, pretend you're a basketball player, and shoot the toothpick into the trash can with perfect form. Watch as the others join in. Start keeping score. Announce the tallies loudly. Watch how fast the meatballs start to disappear. When you get down to the last meatball, don't be gracious. Take it. There's no place for passive-aggressiveness in sports. Eat it. And this time, run over to the trash can with two exaggerated steps, empty toothpick raised above the head, like a soldier. Slam dunk it like a beast and turn around, arms in the air- you just won the game for your team at the buzzer. Talk smack loudly. "This is *my* house!" you proclaim as you beat your chest. Chin-check the opponents. Pour celebratory champagne. You are here. You are the winner. You are victorious. You are the Grand Champion Slam Dunking Meatball Eating Machine, and people better recognize. Now *that's* the best way to eat these meatballs.

CHAPTER TWO

POSSE

In my dreams I had a posse

and they were ride or die.

We terrorized the terrorists.

Teeth sharp. Fists high.

We cursed out the cursers

in our Asian tongues.

We bathed in glorious justice

though we were told there was none.

We shouted the names of the guilty

into the dark air cold.

Pounded the doors of the Baptist Church,

then told them where they could go.

In my dreams I had a posse

and they were ride or die.

We terrorized the terrorists.

Teeth sharp. Fists high.

THE GIRLS ON THE BUS GO ROUND AND ROUND

I don't remember much before Kindergarten. At some point we had moved out of the trailer and into a modest brick house that was located down a gravel road outside of the city limits of Troy, a town about twice the size of Woodland Mills. There were no stoplights, no fast food restaurants and no convenience stores. There was one town doctor. I remember his waiting room walls being lined with oversized rocking chairs that required a step stool if I wanted to sit in one. The nearest grocery store was ten miles away. Although we were lacking in accessible amenities, there was one thing my town had plenty of, and that was churches. There must have been over twenty churches of different denominations, many with less than a hundred regular attendees. It made no sense to me. That's just the way it was.

I was five years old. It was the first day of Kindergarten. I stood at the end of our long driveway, alone. I had never ridden a school bus before. Today was to be my first time. There are no instructions to riding a school bus. You get on when you're supposed to get on. You get off when you're supposed to get off. That's it. But what about what happens in between? No one gave me instructions for that. I was scared. I felt like something bad was going to happen.

I heard a loud, angry engine accelerating down the road and around the corner, even though I couldn't see it yet. I knew what it was. The bus was coming. I turned around to look toward the house to see if my mother or younger sister were watching to wave goodbye to me. I saw no one. I took a deep breath and exhaled out of my nose. I saw a flicker of yellow peeking out of the shallow woods across the road. As the bus got closer, the trees started to fade away and more of the yellow coloring from the bus became clearer and clearer. The bus stopped at the stop sign about a hundred and fifty yards down the road, and made the left turn to come my direction. Now in full view was a huge, deep yellow, angry-sounding bus with a mission to come get me. The closer it got to me, the louder it got and the bigger it looked. It felt like a dinosaur had just emerged from the woods and was now charging towards me with all its might. I kept my feet planted firmly at the end of the driveway, right where my mom had shown me the day before. I didn't move an inch. Just when I thought it looked like the bus was about to swallow me whole, it stopped. The door unfolded open with a squeaking, scraping sound. An old man that looked like he could have been a hundred and thirty-two years old stretched his neck out and looked hard into my eyes like I was an exotic zoo animal he was trying to classify. I stood frozen during this visual examination, waiting for whatever was coming next. After some time, his eyes blinked as if he remembered where he was and he brought his neck back to a more natural position on his body.

"Ya' gonna git eeyan?" He asked in the local dialect. I tried to speak, but nothing came out. I stepped up the first step, which seemed higher than a step should be, and kept stepping up until there weren't any more to climb. I made the left turn to face the seats. The bus was full of people. I didn't know anybody. No one looked my age. Everyone looked like they were in junior high or high school. Some of them looked like grown adults. I remember being told that the elementary students, the junior high students and the high school students all rode the bus at the same time. Then I remembered that I was supposed to make sure that I didn't get off the bus at the high school, like some kids would be doing. I got a hot, terrifying feeling inside my chest.

"Hurry up'n sit down!" the bus driver yelled at me.

I took a few steps forward knowing that the entire bus was looking at me like I didn't belong there. Older girls with crunchy, spiral-permed hair and teased bangs that stood straight up looked at me like I should know better than to try to sit by them. No one invited me to sit down, so the bus driver yelled at one of these girls, forcing her to move over so he could continue on with his route. She huffed and rolled her eyes when I sat down. Her friends, who were in other seats around her, taking up as much space as possible, glared at me like I was a rat that had infested their school bus empire.

My jet black hair was parted down the middle and French braided on each side of my head from the front of my forehead all the way to the end. My braids were tied with elastics that had clear red spheres as decorations- a hairstyle that wasn't very fashionable at the time. I wore a skirt that went past my knees, a tucked in shirt that was buttoned to my throat, and simple brown loafers. My backpack was solid navy, made from durable canvas material. This wasn't a fun look for a five year old in Kindergarten in the 80's, especially since my school didn't require a uniform. The girl sitting beside me seemed to be able to communicate very clearly with the other girls on the bus just by looking at them. She slowly began inching her way closer and closer to me, causing the green vinyl space on the seat that was separating us to slowly shrink. I sat perfectly still, once again waiting for whatever was about to happen. Eventually she was so close that almost no space was between us at all. I looked down to avoid eye contact with her. I could see our arms close to each other. Hers had more hair. My half Filipino skin that had been baking in the summer sun was so much darker than her creamy, pinky shade of porcelain skin. Then I realized it. I was the darkest girl on the bus, and I was the littlest.

"So, what are you?" the girl said in a menacing tone, almost in a whisper.

"What do you mean?" I asked without looking at her.

"You know what I mean," she said.

"No, I don't." I continued staring at my shoes. She popped her gum loudly in my ear.

"Are you stupid?" she asked. "I want to know what you are."

"I don't know what you mean," I said. I could feel her frustration growing and the other girls watching this conversation with quiet pleasure on their faces, waiting for something to happen that I was sure they would find entertaining. These girls were mean, and they liked being mean together.

"Are you a Jap?" she asked me.

"What's a Jap?" I asked honestly.

"Japanese, stupid! Are you Japanese? Do you eat with chopsticks and stuff?" The other girls began laughing.

"No," I said.

"Are you an Eskimo?" she asked, taunting me. Another girl chimed in from across the aisle and said, "She can't be an Eskimo. It's hot outside." Clearly, intelligence was not these girls' forte.

"No," I said quietly, just wanting the bus ride to be over.

She put her lips close to my cheek. I could smell the Juicy Fruit chewing gum on her breath and the White Rain hairspray in her hair. I knew she was about to say something mean.

"Then you must be a nigger," she said, pleased with herself. The other girls laughed like it was the moment they had been waiting for since I got on the bus.

"I don't know what that means," I said. The girls looked at each other in confusion, like they didn't know whether or not to believe me.

"How come you don't know what a nigger is when you are one?" another girl asked. I looked at her blankly. I had never heard that word before.

"She really don't know, y'all," another one said. "Leave her alone, she's stupid."

"Yeah, she's stupid. They should take her to Kingdom," said another one. There was an explosion of laughter. I didn't know what Kingdom was either.

The girl sitting beside me was still looking hard into my face, sitting so close that anyone looking would have thought she was either about to kiss my cheek or bite it. I could still smell her gum and hairspray. I felt her exhale out of her nose and slide back towards the window, like a slithering dragon that decided to retreat because the meal wasn't worth the effort. The atmosphere relaxed and I could breathe easier, but all of the girls still kept their eyes on me for the rest of the ride.

The bus driver pulled up to my little elementary school comprised of two small buildings and a few trailers. Yes, trailers. The elementary school in Troy, Tennessee, used trailers for some of their classrooms in 1982. I stood up to get off the bus and walked towards the front. I got close to where the bus driver was, with a little bitterness towards him because he didn't keep a better watch over the kids' behavior while he was driving. I knew he was too old. It was a miracle straight from God that he could drive the bus at all and get us to school without crashing.

"Don't forget now, you're a nigger! Ya' hear that? A nigger!" someone shouted. There was another explosion of laughter. The driver looked at them in his huge rear view mirror that was above his head, but said nothing. I guessed it must have been true, whatever it was.

I stepped off of the bus and knew that what I had just experienced was the world that I would have to face before 8AM every school morning on my way to Kindergarten. There was no point in telling my parents. My father had to be at work at Goodyear before the bus came in the morning, and my mother didn't know how to drive. There was nothing they could do about it, so there was no point in telling them. I wanted to cry, but I knew it wouldn't do any good. I was about to face my Kindergarten classroom for the first time and I wanted to make friends. I didn't want to be known as the cry baby, so during the long walk to the classroom I pushed down my tears, along with the confusion, hurt, and shame. I tried my best to forget about it, even though I already knew I would have to repeat that same experience in twenty four hours. I decided to go to class and to be so nice that people couldn't be mean to me.

"You're five years old," I told myself. "You have to be

a big girl now."

Beef Bulgogi & Cucumber Kimchi Wraps

YIELD: Posse of 4-6

PREP STEPS:
- Make cucumber kimchi, 12-24 hours ahead
- Make bulgogi marinade, 10 minutes
- Marinate the meat, 30 minutes
- Cook the bulgogi, 7-10 minutes (depending on your preference)
- Make the wraps (time depends on your wrapping skills)

KIMCHI:
- 3 small cucumbers
- 1 tsp. kosher salt
- 3 cloves garlic, finely chopped
- 2 scallions, white and light green parts, chopped to desired size
- 1¼-inch piece fresh ginger, peeled and finely chopped
- 2 Tbs. rice vinegar
- 1 Tbs. crushed red pepper
- 2½ tsp. sugar
- 1/2 tsp. fish sauce

Cut the cucumbers in half lengthwise and then crosswise into moons of your preferred thickness. Place in a bowl and mix with the salt. Side aside at room temperature for about 30 minutes while you combine the garlic, scallions, ginger, vinegar, chili powder, sugar and fish sauce in a separate bowl (don't use metal). Drain the liquid that the cucumbers rendered. Pour the cucumbers into the vinegar mixture and stir gently 2-3 times. Cover and refrigerate for 12 to 24 hours before making wraps.

BEEF BULGOGI:

- 2 lbs. of boneless rib-eye or flank steak, sliced thinly
- 1 small yellow onion, sliced in half, then into half moons
- 2 scallions, sliced into 2 inch pieces
- 1-2 Tbs. canola oil for pan frying

BULGOGI MARINADE:

- ⅓ cup of soy sauce
- 3 Tbs. white sugar
- 1 Tbs. toasted sesame oil
- 6 garlic cloves, minced or grated
- 3 tsp. ginger, minced or grated

- 2 tsp. ground black pepper

Trim the meat of fat and slice it as thinly as possible, slicing against the grain. Combine the marinade ingredients in a large bowl. Once the sugar has dissolved, add the beef, scallion and onion slices to the bowl. Let sit for 30 minutes. Heat large skillet over medium high heat and add the oil. Using tongs, remove beef and onions from marinade (shaking off excess) and cook in oil until done to your preference (5 minutes for medium-rare).

WRAPS:
- 1 head butter lettuce, leaves separated, washed and dried
- 2-3 cups cooked rice (your choice)
- 1 scallion, finely sliced
- 3 Tbs. toasted sesame seeds
- cooked beef bulgogi
- kimchi

ASSEMBLY & EATING:

Lay out a piece of foil about 1.5 times bigger than the size of the lettuce leaf you'll be using. Place the lettuce leaf in the center of the foil. Layer some rice, then bulgogi (the juice of the meat will penetrate the rice, so this method is best in my opinion). Layer the cucumber kimchi on top of the meat and sprinkle with sesame seeds. Choose your own amounts for all the fillings. Don't be too serious about it. Wrap the lettuce burrito style, then wrap the foil around it to encase the entire wrap for travel. Keep making more until you run out of everything.

Night will come. Your parents will go to bed. What are you waiting for? Swipe your dad's car keys. Put the car in neutral so it rolls out of the driveway silently. When you are far enough away from the house so that starting the engine won't wake them, crank her up. Meet your friends at the place where they know to be waiting. When they jump in the car, smile that one smile you smile. Roll up your sleeves and roll down the windows. Scream to the stars while you hold your friend's hand. Turn up a Gwen Stefani song. Sing. Sing louder. Then sing it again. Take pictures and send somebody one. Moments like these are rare. And when your bodies are famished from singing to the night sky, pull the car over on your favorite secluded backroad. Turn off the headlights so there aren't any red flags. What are you waiting for? Toss the wraps to your girls. Tap the tops of them with each other like they are unbreakable wine glasses filled with choice wine. Fold the top of the foil down. Take a bite. Taste the yummy. You are free. You are beautiful. You are cool. You are not a rich girl, but you are luxurious. You have found your sweet escape at four in the morning. Don't get it twisted- these friends are the real thing. There's no more misery. It's a wonderful life and that's the truth.

CHAPTER THREE

LIGHT CARRIER

An imminent dark day now shines brightly.

By what means does light cover

such a long distance in such a short time?

What wind, what sail,

what angel carried it in her wings?

What crosses distance so quickly

that time takes a back seat?

BIG TROUBLE IN LITTLE KINDERGARTEN

I was late. I can't remember why. I just remember that when I arrived and stood in the door of my classroom, the other students were playing with different toys and they all seemed to know each other. My mom had paid special attention getting me ready for school that day. It was decided that I would wear a skirt and a matching top. Skirt days were always full of dread to me as a youngster. There was the ceremonious "tucking ritual" that felt torturous and unnecessary but had to occur so no one "could see anything they shouldn't," as my mom would say. Out of the shower, she put my underwear on first. Then the shirt...which got tucked into the underwear, then pantyhose which were placed on top of the underwear that the shirt was tucked into, then shorts on top of the pantyhose. And finally came the skirt. I was certain no other human wore a skirt in this manner. I felt like an Asian oompa loompa. I remember thinking, "I hope I don't have to go pee. I'll never put this back in the right order." I had nightmarish visions of walking into the classroom with my panties on top of all of my clothes.

As soon as I put one foot in the classroom, all the kids stopped what they were doing and turned to stare at me. I remember one boy with hair so blonde it looked white. He peered from around a bookcase, where a picture of President Ronald Regan was hanging, to see why everyone had stopped playing and got quiet.

When he saw me, his mouth fell open. He looked over at the teacher and said in a backwoods southern accent, "Wail, what eeyen the wer-rold is THAT supposed to be? Am I gonna be in class with some nigger?" There was that word again. How did everyone know this word except me? If anything, I thought I would know more words than everyone else because I was used to hearing my mom speak Tagalog in addition to English, but I was wrong. I had never heard this "nigger" word before.

My heart sank for a reason I couldn't exactly explain. The teacher gave him a look like she would deal with him later. She came over and held my hand and walked me to my place at one of the tables. She sat me beside another girl with black hair whose skin was slightly lighter than mine. Her name was Julie. She was the prettiest girl in the class and she seemed to know the teacher very well. I remember thinking that her mom must be a teacher too. I didn't expect Julie to like me. It appeared she already had friends, and surely after what just happened, she wouldn't want to add me as one more. I decided to keep to myself. Later that day the teacher told the class to draw a tree on a piece of paper using any colors we wanted, and to put our name at the bottom of our artwork. When it was time to lift our heads and show our work to the teacher, Julie and I looked at each other's trees to discover that they looked identical. They were the same shape, with roots drawn growing into the dirt, and we had used the same colors in the same places. We first gasped, and then we smiled at each other. I had made my first friend. I thought I'd ask her if she wanted to go beat up the high school girls on the bus with me, but I decided it was too soon for that. After that, Julie and I sat beside each other every day. We helped each other do our work. We stood in line for lunch together and played on the playground. She told me to stop tucking my shirt into my panties like a weirdo. Making friends with her was the best thing that happened to me in Kindergarten. It even made the bus ride to school a little more bearable.

Flight of Coconut Milk Hot Chocolates: White, Peppermint & Dark

YIELD: 1 flight of 3 hot chocolates each for 4 people.

- 1 cup white chocolate chips
- 1 cup semi-sweet chocolate chips
- 1 cup Andes Peppermint Crunch Baking Chips
- 3 cups canned coconut milk (not coconut cream)
- 12 cups coconut almond milk (can be found in the milk section)
- Freshly grated nutmeg to garnish (or a dash of dried)
- Cocoa powder to garnish
- Cinnamon sticks or grated cinnamon for garnish

Note: Make one flavor at a time, each in different saucepans.

Melt white chocolate chips in a saucepan with 1 cup of the canned coconut milk. Stir over medium heat until it is warmed together. Stir in 4 cups of the coconut almond milk and heat to the desired temperature. For the remaining two flavors, repeat the process in clean saucepans, following the same method and recipe, with semisweet chips in one pan and peppermint chips in the other.

ASSEMBLY & DRINKING:

I find this is a fun recipe to serve at a party because people never expect to get a flight of hot chocolate. This is a drink that is best served when the party has gone into the night hours and the bonfire in the back yard is at its strongest. Usually, there is a lost bag of marshmallows that won't be found until the sun rises, and the kids have secretly eaten most of the chocolate during the daytime when the parents weren't looking. At the parties I host, people constantly go back and forth from the house. We don't sit politely at the dinner table. Our music is a little too loud for the neighbors, but at least we have good taste. Besides, they are always invited anyway. For these reasons, I have found that it is wisest to serve these in brown paper cups made for coffee- another surprise for a "flight" of anything. I carry a large tray of all the flavors outside to a table, and arrange a "flight buffet" of sorts: four rows with three different flavors in each row. I arrange a wicker basket with rolled up napkins and shakers full of cinnamon and nutmeg. I lay my microplane that is too fancy to be outside across the whole basket with a small container that holds fresh nutmeg in whole form. I place several cinnamon sticks in the basket and sprinkle a few loose flowers all around, just for decoration. When it's dark outside and everyone is exhausted, it is my opinion that it is nice to offer something fresh and lovely to the guests. Inevitably people will come to the table, where I'll be standing nearby to see if anyone needs anything. One of the rowdier family members will pick up one of the cups and make some snippy (but loving) comment about how unnecessarily fancy I am. He'll look at me with a grin as he places the cup to his mouth and turns it bottom side up, as if he had just "won" something in the conversation by being rude and unappreciative. I just stand politely with my arms folded with a smile on my face while thinking, "Uh huh…but you sure are drinking the heck out of my hot chocolate."

CHAPTER FOUR

Run

Terror hit them like a ghost in the face,

guilt from the sin in their pocket disgraced.

The ones that fled, their tracks she did trace,

then sent them to the judge on the plagioclase.

The gems and the jewels once held in their hands

lay lonely on the ground on God's green land.

To wilt, to whither, to turn to dust,

no hope for life, no room for rust.

Run! Run! Run! For judgment is near,

but in case the cat hasn't told you,

we're all mad here.

PECANS ON THE PLAYGROUND

I was always one of those kids at school who never knew what they were going to do during recess. Sometimes I would play with a small group of friends so hard that I would need to get several drinks of water before it was time to come in, but other times I would sit by myself, and I was just fine with that. On those days, I sat alone on one of the playground's many hills. I particularly enjoyed a spot under a big oak tree that was off to the side of one of the school buildings and away from the playground traffic. Kids never ran around this tree and it was always shady. My favorite thing to do was to look down the hill and across a flat patch of grass to the building where the third grade classrooms were located. Beyond that building was a deep ditch that had flowing water in it. There was no fence to save any child who wandered too closely and lost his or her footing. For that reason, students weren't allowed to play near it, but from where I sat under my little tree, every now and then I got a glimpse of a student who had taken the risk of sneaking down there to pocket the prize pecans that fell off the huge pecan tree. In the fall, the fallen pecans lay on the ground in open piles for the picking. When this happened, a child sneaking off to this forbidden territory was a common occurrence, maybe two or three times a week. Thanks to my personal shade tree being positioned at the perfect angle, I had exclusive show seating. Each time I had the stressful joy of watching this happen, I would be as nervous as if I was witnessing a prisoner try to escape from Alcatraz right before my eyes. Sometimes they would get away free and leave with a pocket full of pecans, but usually I'd see the door of one of the third grade classrooms open with ferocity. Miss Hilda, a tall stick-figure of an older woman with very short grey hair and thick ironed blue jeans, would run across the field towards the convict as if he might jump the moat and never be seen again. It was better than Saturday morning cartoons, and I laughed every time. Then I'd watch as the child would be instructed to empty his pockets. Then Miss Hilda would point up the hill which meant he was to walk to the principal's office in his pecan-stealing shame. Inevitably he would get a "paddling" from the principal, which meant he was going to get spanked on the rear with large wooden board specially crafted for such a job. When I was in the third grade there was a rumor that the principal had taken his paddle somewhere special to have it upgraded from a basic plank of wood to an electric paddle, which now delivered a shock upon being spanked that was just a few volts lower than the electric chair. There is never a shortage of rumors in a small town.

It took me three school years to muster up the guts to try my own pecan heist. I had watched other kids do it so many times that I knew where the flaws were in their attempts. I knew I could do it and do it well. One day after school, I came home with enough pecans for my mom to make not one, but *two* pecan pies! The house filled with the scent of bubbling brown sugar and warm, toasty pecans. I walked around the house proudly strutting while taking credit for the pecan provision of two pecan pies that day! We all enjoyed pie after dinner that evening. I believe I ate an extra piece. And why not? I deserved it! After all, I brought the pecans home!

After our stomachs were full, I was so pleased to see we still had another whole pecan pie for the next day. As I was eyeing it over with prideful fantasies of stretching out my victory strut over two days instead of one, my mother suggested that I take the extra pie to my teacher, who happened to be... Miss Hilda, the lady I had watched serve as pecan patrol for over three years.

"Dalena, you gib dis pie to your teacha'," my mother said in her accent.

My stomach sank. The fear hit me. I thought I would vomit pecan pie for the rest of my life. I walked into my third grade class the next day with my mother's foil-covered pecan pie in hand. I had taken such special care not to damage it on the school bus that morning that I didn't even notice the mean girls' existence that day. All I did the entire bus ride was sit perfectly still and stare down at it, like the pie was a newborn baby that might stop breathing at any moment. It looked perfect when I handed it to her.

"Oh, what's this?" asked Miss Hilda.

"Pecan pie," I said squeamishly.

She casually put her hands on the pie to take it and then she froze. She stared at me while putting the pieces of the story together in her mind, but I couldn't bear it, so I looked to the ground...in my pecan-stealing shame. Miss Hilda didn't know whether to scold me or laugh. She sent me back to my desk. All day she would be in the middle of a lesson, start laughing under her breath, and then gracefully compose herself while hiding her face in the huge world map that she had pulled down over the chalkboard. Other teachers would knock on the door periodically and Miss Hilda would excuse herself from the classroom and bring the pie with her. We could hear soft giggles from outside of the room where she was obviously recounting the story with her visual aid, which was my baked to perfection in my mother's oven the day before. It was the first time someone had been caught stealing pecans without being sent to the principal's office to be spanked with the infamous electric paddle. Miss Hilda never had to tell me that I wasn't allowed to play near the pecan tree again. I just never did, but all of my other teachers after the third grade almost encouraged me to. Now I know it's because they wanted some of my mother's pecan pie. But they were out of luck. I had washed my hands of having "sticky fingers" and I put my pecan thieving days behind me. A pecan never touched my hands again, at least not from Troy Elementary.

Thief's Pecan Pie

YIELD: 1 (9-inch) pie

CRUST:

- 1 cup all-purpose flour
- ½ cup Crisco
- 1/3 of a whisked egg (about 1 Tbs.)
- 1½ Tbs. cold water
- 1 tsp. white vinegar
- 1/2 tsp. of salt

Combine the flour and Crisco in a large mixing bowl and press together for 2-3 minutes with a pastry cutter or fork, until everything is combined and it looks like crumbly Play-Doh. Add the Tbs. of whisked egg, water, vinegar and salt. Mix together lightly. Don't beat it or squeeze it, just get it all mixed together. Sprinkle a little flour on your rolling surface and rolling pin and get to rolling. Don't be nervous. (Most of the crust is on the bottom of the pie, so no one will know if she's had a hard day.) Roll out the dough to 9½ inches across (you'll need the extra for the lip of the pan). When the crust is large enough and pretty uniform in thickness, lift and place into a 9" pie pan. Carefully press crust into the sides of the pan. When I do this, I use the same pressure as when I powder my nose. You can decorate the edges with any crimping technique you like. I usually don't worry about it too much as long as it looks clean.

FILLING:

- 1½ cups pecan pieces
- 3 eggs, at room temperature
- ¾ cup sugar
- ¾ cup light corn syrup
- 2 Tbs. melted butter
- 2 tsp. vanilla extract
- ½ tsp. salt
- 8-10 grates fresh nutmeg

Lay out the pecans in a single layer onto a baking sheet and bake at 350 degrees for 8 minutes or until toasted. Remove from the oven and allow to cool for 10 minutes. Stir remaining filling ingredients together in a large bowl. Add pecans to the mixture and combine thoroughly. Pour filling into pie shell. Bake at 350 degrees. After twenty minutes, loosely cover top of pie with foil. Bake for another 30-40 minutes or until the pie is set. Remove pie from oven, remove the foil and let rest for 15 minutes, then it's done.

ASSEMBLY & EATING:

Sometimes I wonder if I'm just super sloppy or super lazy, but I always feel like I deserve a major award after baking this pie. I feel that way because I have to deal with my destroyed kitchen. You probably won't have to do the same. This is actually a very traditional, very simple recipe and it's not a messy one at all, especially if you clean as you go. It's just that over the years, I've made peace with my sloppiness when dealing with flour and dough-rolling. Yes, I admit it; I don't cook like these Pinterest and Instagram cooks with their perfect kitchens and vases of fresh flowers that never seem to wilt. I cook like a warrior charging through the woods, looking for her buried sword to kill the enemy across the way. And then when the baking pecan pie starts filling up my kitchen with the smell of nuts, sugar, and yummy goo, a peace comes over me that brings me back to myself and I have to sit. And sit. And sit. I snap out of my contemplative stare only by the timer going off to remind me to take the pie out of the oven. I was doing it again...I was thinking about those pecans on the playground, but now I think about it from an adult perspective. Why didn't the teachers harvest the nuts themselves on the weekend? Why *couldn't* the students take them home? Were they determined for the pecans to go to waste? As an adult I still don't understand. And I don't understand why my mind would devote time to wondering about such irrelevant things years and years later, but it does. At any rate, I put a slice of pecan pie in the left side of my bowl and I place a scoop of vanilla ice cream beside it on the right, not on top. From left to right in my bowl, this allows me to have some pecan pie unaffected by ice cream, some pecan pie saturated by ice cream, some ice cream infiltrated by pecan pie, and some ice cream unaffected by pecan pie. Instead of one dessert, I now have four- all in the same bowl. Consider yourself formally introduced to my dessert genius. This is, in my estimation, the only way to eat this beloved pecan pie, while of course, not caring one bit if your floor is still dusted with fallen flour, like mine will be the next time I make it. No one cares. Just eat the pie, already.

CHAPTER FIVE

POEM FOR BILLY

Gag a mag and yuck yuck yuck

Spit and spat the choke got stuck

Foiled by his foolish pride

Peanut gallery on the side

Tension tight and people betting

Gag me with a full place setting

Heart so frozen, cold as snow

Way too tough, no yeast in your dough

Sour stomach, bitter tongue

Your home so hard when you were young

I hope you turned and chose the light

Skin is skin, all shades are right

Where's Billy now, the name we don't hear?

Are you married and happy? Are you living in fear?

Are you a spirit, a spark, a petty morel?

I pray for you Billy. I hope you are well.

THE EMPRESS STRIKES BACK

There was another place at school that was destined to provide me and those around me with great entertainment. That place was the school cafeteria... especially days when I brought my own lunch. I didn't find that many kids flocked to me in the classroom or during recess, but in the cafeteria, I was a boss. From the moment we would stand in line as fourth graders to walk to the lunch room, my classmates would bend forward looking in my direction to see if I had brought my own lunch that day. If I did, I would see kids start to elbow each other down the line and people would begin striking deals in order to get closer to me so they would be sitting in my proximity when I took out my leftovers from last night's dinner to eat.

"Hey Tina! I'll give you three of my glitter pencils if you let me switch with you." Glitter pencils and puffy stickers were kid currency of choice in the fourth grade. "I have enough glitter pencils, Brian," she'd say with a bit of attitude.

"Ooohhhhhh!" the class would say together in a burning response.

Even though I knew their reason for wanting to sit by me was so they could act grossed out when I showed them my lunch, I giggled a little from the attention and their lack of experience with foods from other cultures. After everyone went through the line to get their plastic tray of mass prepared food and we found our seats at the lunch table, the show would begin. I would place my brown paper sack on the table. (I had long outgrown my Strawberry Shortcake tin lunchbox that I carried when I was younger.) Slowly I would unroll the top of the bag. Then I would snap open the top of it as if I were the Phantom of the Opera opening his cape. I'd look in the eyes of everyone around me as they sat frozen by my wondrous lunch bag-opening abilities. I'd reach down with one of my hands. The surfacing vessel contained unknown food which still remained a mystery. Eyes grew wider and wider as it began to peek out of the top of the bag. Once it was on the table, I removed the bag and moved it to the floor as not to obstruct my audience's view. Gasps were imminent. After letting their imaginations run wild with the possible contents, I began to inch the lid off like a burlesque dancer taking off one of her long satin gloves. Right before completely pulling the lid off, I would announce the contents like the host on Iron Chef America.

"SPAM FRIED RICE!"

"Ewww!" they would respond in exaggerated unity, looking at each other in agreement. My lunchtime show only lasted a few weeks. Miss Susie, a teacher from another class, had seen my audience's reaction and decided it was too much of a distraction. She believed that I needed to eat my lunch without a show-stopping performance, like a commoner. "What you eat is your business," she said. Although she sadly ended my stint on the lunchroom stage, it perpetuated my popularity in the school. Soon, the fact that I was half-Caucasian American and half-Filipino had spread into a rumor about me being everything from a slave to an empress from far away unexplored lands, like the planet Mars or... Hawaii, and it came to be told that I kept all sorts of "creepy crawlies" in my lunch box to eat. One of my classmates, Billy, wasn't having it. Billy was a beast. He had failed fourth grade... twice. He was a lot bigger than everybody and he was mean. He would constantly get in the worst kind of trouble. He was always being sent to the principal's office for cheating, cussing and spitting. One time he was gone for two weeks because he got sent to "Juvenile." I didn't know what "Juvenile" was exactly, but I knew he was sent there for trying to hit a teacher. He had a lot of friends in the older grades and he acted more like a teenager than a kid at all. Billy wreaked havoc in my classroom. He stole people's pencils, chalk, and any good thing someone might happen to bring, like a new eraser. He would pull the girls' hair, call us vulgar names and hit the boys when the teacher had her back turned to the class. He was also the type that acted like nothing impressed him because whatever cool and awesome thing you were talking about, he had already experienced himself and knew all about it. At least that's what he wanted everyone to believe. I knew Billy was a liar, plus he had made fun of me and hurt my friends one too many times. One day after lunch on the playground I decided I had had enough.

"Billy! Billy! You won't believe it! Dalena brought clear noodles in her lunchbox today!" the kids told him.

"Yeah, so what? I eat them all the time," he said barely looking up to acknowledge the conversation.

Now, I didn't need anyone to be impressed with my lunch, but I was fed up with him being a "one-upper" and discounting everyone's experiences and stories. I knew no one in my school knew anything about clear noodles. Maybe it was the years of dealing with the mean girls on the bus. Maybe it was the years of not having one person in my life who could understand what it was like to be me. Whatever it was, it all came together that day in a brave decision to call Billy's bluff without fear of what would happen next.

"You eat caterpillar noodles too?" I asked loudly, making sure everyone could hear me. Billy stood up and stumbled over his words.

"Uh. Uh. Well yeah, it's no big deal," he said, trying to recover. There was an awkward silence of anticipation as a crowd grew.

"Dalena, those were *caterpillar* noodles?" someone asked me.

"That's right," I said, fearlessly putting my hands on my hips and looking Billy straight in the eyes. "Noodles made out of caterpillars." Everyone started to get grossed out, but then I said, "I wanted to bring straight caterpillars to eat but the teachers said I couldn't." At this point my closest friends knew what I was up to, but many onlookers didn't. I never took my eyes off of Billy, and soon everyone else was looking at him too.

"Billy, have you ever eaten...*caterpillars*?" a little boy asked him, almost afraid to hear the answer. Kids were used to creating and hearing all kinds of false stories about me, my family, what I ate and where I came from. I ignored them all. This was the first story about me that they were hearing straight from my own mouth. Billy was lost.

"Um, yeah. Of course I have. It's no big deal. It's just a caterpillar. I eat 'em all the time," he said thinking he would sound impressive.

"Ewwwwwww!" everyone screamed in disgust. He was so used to saying his rhetoric and people responding positively that he never suspected to get this reaction. Billy looked at me like he would kill me.

"Here Billy! Here's a caterpillar!" Someone ran up to him with a little black worm with little feet dangling between their index finger and thumb. Even I got nervous, but I just kept looking at Billy. My poker face could have won me a thousand dollars that day.

Soon kids started chanting "Bill-EE, Bill-EE, Bill-EE!" to encourage him to eat it. I stared at him knowing this was the time of truth. He could either put his pride down and finally admit that he was just a big fat faker, or... he could eat a caterpillar. Billy looked around at the crowd and then back at me. I couldn't believe he was actually considering eating it. This had gone too far too fast. But it was too late, we were both in it to win it. Never in my life have I ever eaten a bug, and certainly a caterpillar wouldn't be my first choice if I had to. Poor Billy couldn't put his pride down. He opened his mouth, looked at me like I was the devil, and dropped the caterpillar in with his eyes shut so tight I thought he was going to swallow his eyeballs too. He swallowed hard and then opened his eyes. After about two seconds of silence, at least three people lost their lunch and everyone else made the most horrific sounds of disgust ever to hit Troy Elementary. Billy looked at me and yelled, "I HATE YOU!" He was so mad that some of the onlookers had gone to fetch a teacher because they were scared he was going to hit me. Miss Susie arrived on the scene quickly. She grabbed my wrist and turned me around in a manner that would get her fired in today's day and age. "Did Billy eat a caterpillar because you said you did?" she asked horrifically. I took a breath and thought for a moment about what to say.

"What he eats is his business," I said to her. She was fit to be tied. I thought steam was going to come out of her ears like a cartoon character. She took Billy's hand, who was now crying like a baby, and walked him away from the crowd to console him. As they walked up the hill, I could see a few other teachers who were swallowing their laughter and covering their mouths. No one could believe I took on Billy and won. If anyone had told us in the morning that we would see Billy eat a caterpillar and cry that day, people would have said it was impossible. If anyone would have said that *I* would be the reason for it, that would've seemed even more impossible. I got to be the hero for about three days at school. The story and my name traveled all the way up to the eighth grade. Every now and then I would catch some older boys standing in a group, looking at me and smiling. "That's her. That's her," they'd say. For a while I became known as "the girl who made Billy eat a caterpillar and cry." I made an effort to not gloat in it too much, but the teachers who looked at me like they were just a little proud made it difficult on some days. I was just thankful he stopped being so bad at school. As an adult now, I can look back and say with certainty that Billy probably had a very difficult home life and I feel badly for him. Even so, you can't go around bullying people. From what I remember, Billy didn't steal, hit or make fun of anyone else for the rest of the year, and I got to eat my caterpillar noodles in peace.

Ham Hock Pancit

YIELD: 6-8 servings

- 2 cups ham hocks, boiled in water or stock until falling off the bone, drained, patted dry and sliced thinly
- 1 (12 ounce) package bean thread noodles
- 1 (16 ounce) package coleslaw mix (shredded cabbage and carrots)
- 1 small onion, finely diced
- 4 cloves garlic, minced
- 2 Tbs. vegetable oil
- 2 Tbs. soy sauce
  Optional:
  2 tsp. fish sauce
  Lemon wedges or for squeezing and garnish

Place the rice noodles in a large bowl with enough warm water to cover the noodles. When soft, drain and set aside. Heat oil in a large skillet over medium heat. Sauté onion and garlic until the onion begins to soften. Add ham hock slices, cabbage mix and soy sauce. Stir until the cabbage begins to soften. Add the noodles and stir until heated through. (If adding fish sauce, do so at this point and stir again). Cover and let rest for 5 minutes to marry the flavors before serving.

ASSEMBLY & EATING:

Pancit is a traditional Filipino noodle dish. It's as common in the Philippines as french fries are in America. Everyone has their special way of making it, and usually they all like their own familiar versions of their mother's or one of their auntie's the best. The recipe I'm sharing here is very simple and I introduce a southern shortcut by using a bag of coleslaw mix for the pre-shredded cabbage and carrots, instead of spending time shredding cabbage and carrots by hand. If you're a traditional Filipino cook, my suggestion in the previous sentence probably just made you gasp, and visions of me needing to go to church to get "pancit short-cut forgiveness" probably flashed in your mind.

"Use a bag of shredded cabbage and carrots from the store? Why would you do that? How will your family know you love them if you don't meticulously and laboriously shred half a head of cabbage and 4 large carrots by hand with the tiniest razor blade you can find?" you ask.

I know, I know. Filipinos, along with many other cultures, traditionally show their love by how hard they have worked in the kitchen. Chances are, if you are from a large family you can usually pinpoint a few people who parade their hard work on their faces with an exaggerated look of exhaustion and worry because they want a few extra pats on the back. That's just not my style. I don't believe that exhaustion and worry equal love. I'm not trying to get all political. All I'm saying is, if you're tired and you want to make pancit, consider using a bag of pre-shredded cabbage and carrots. I promise the police won't arrest you. After your pancit is cooked, reach up to the top shelf above your plates and get out your pancit dish- the turquoise Cinderella bowl with the white flowers and the tight lid that weighs four pounds. Transfer the pancit into the bowl. Slice the lemon wedges in fourths and arrange them in a circle pattern in the bowl. Pancit can dry out and get stale in open air, so cover it with the lid until it's time to eat. Go to the bathroom and wash your hands. Wash your face. Look in the mirror. Curl your hair around your fingers a bit. Pinch your cheeks to encourage a little color. Spray yourself with something that smells nice. Smile. Be happy. Be energetic. Your family loves you because of you, not because of your hard work. Set yourself free from traditions that tell you that the more miserable you act, the more people will appreciate you. It's a lie. Put on some red lipstick.

Answer the door. Thank God. You have people. Eat pancit.

CHAPTER SIX

THE SCIENCE OF BRAINWASHING

Words of the unwise
injected into her mind,
twisting and tinkering,
fine-tuning her thinking,
changing her
from who
she was meant to be,
into a version of the girl
that was fit for he.
Carrying courage and strength,
unaccepting of the length
of time that she was to be
their specimen for testing.
No petri dish resting,
no beaker swish cresting,
no Catholic church blessing,
only words questing,
to change
who she
was meant to be.

THE HOUSE THAT POVERTY BUILT

I think if you could give five random people in the United States a magical looking glass that could allow them to see into my fifth grade classroom, two or three of them would say most of us were poor. We didn't consider ourselves poor- our parents worked, bills got paid, and we had what we needed. We didn't complain about not having name brand clothes or shoes, but we made a big deal if someone happened to have them. Maybe people who went to school with me who are reading this will disagree with that, but I remember our teacher keeping her box of chalk locked in her top drawer because that one box had to last her all year, and I remember that when someone needed to wash their hands, she went to the sink in the back of the classroom with them in order to dispense the tiniest drop from the donated bottle of soap into our hands in order to prolong its life, so you do the poverty math.

Peggy sat in the back of the class in fifth grade. She didn't talk to many people and not many people talked to her. It's weird how there are different levels of poverty among the poor, but there are. In my poor school, I was considered nearly rich because my dad worked at Goodyear. Peggy was considered the opposite, although it's hard to say why. Kids just know, I guess. One day I decided I wanted to be friends with her. I casually said hello as I passed her desk on the way to the sink with the teacher to wash my hands. Peggy leaned away from me like I had sneezed on her. It was okay. I have never gotten offended easily, and I was not one to give up on something I wanted. I was determined that Peggy would have a friend in class, and I was determined that it would be me. Over the next few weeks, I said hi to her at least once a day, sometimes more. At first she was annoyed. Then she seemed amused, and then one day she giggled when I said hi. That was the day we played on the playground together for the first time. We had fun. She had a great laugh. No one had ever seen Peggy play on the playground- she usually sat and watched everyone else, or she would sit at her desk, alone in the classroom, waiting for everyone else to return. School kids stood with their mouths open and watched me and Peggy chasing each other and playing on the see-saw like we were the oddity attraction at the county fair. We didn't care.

Peggy and I became decent playmates at school, and

one day she invited me to come to her house on a Saturday. My dad slowly pulled up her long driveway and looked at the house like it must have been the wrong address. Then he turned his neck to look all around as if maybe her house was nearby and not the one we were looking at…. which stood in the middle of a corn field with no other houses in sight. It was an average sized house for the area, one story with a porch, but it was old. I mean really old. Now take the picture of the old house in your mind and make it even older than that. It looked like people from the Civil War days probably lived there at one time, and it looked like repairs had never been done to it since then. Boards were crooked all over the house. There was junk in the yard and there wasn't any grass. There were old pots and pans and jugs everywhere, and they too had been there a long time, almost embedded into the earth.

"Surely, this can't be it," my dad said.

Then a man stepped out of the front door and onto the porch. He was slowly loading a shell into his shotgun while he looked at us. Then Peggy appeared at his side. She saw me and waved.

"Is that her?" my dad asked.

"Yeah," I said. My dad and I waved back. She tugged on his shirt and said something casually to him and he stopped loading the gun and went back inside the house.

"Well, are you going?" my dad asked me. I was a little scared, but I felt like I didn't have a choice but to stay. After all, I had already agreed to come over. I got out of the truck and my dad drove in reverse out of the long driveway past the rows of corn. I felt uneasy, but I could hear birds singing. I wasn't scared. Peggy ran towards me and we instantly started playing outside. I explored all of the jugs, loose wood and old car parts that were lying around. Peggy giggled at me.

"You're acting like you're in a museum. It's just junk," she said.

"Well, why is it here?" I asked.

"I don't know. It's always been here. Exactly in the same spot," she said.

"Why don't y'all clean it up?" I asked.

"Where would we put it?" she responded.

"I don't know. The trash?"

"Trash don't come out here," she said tossing an old knife into a pile of rubble.

"Then where does your trash go?" I asked.

"We take it to the river," she said.

"You mean you throw your trash into the river?" I was appalled. My dad always taught me to honor the land. There was only one river she could be talking about- the Mississippi. It was about thirty minutes away.

"Yeah," she said. "Once or twice a year we take our trash there and dump it." She said it so casually, it scared me.

"Peggy," I said with an open mouth and breaking heart, "you shouldn't do that." She threw a rock into the corn field.

"Eh, Ma and Dad says it's no big deal cause there's plenty of water." I wanted to go home. I didn't understand what kind of place this was or how people could think like this. I didn't know how long I had left to be there, but I didn't want to be there anymore. Still, I felt sorry for Peggy so I tried to play and have fun, but it was hard.

We got thirsty so we went to the side of the house to get a drink from the water hose. I have always loved drinking out of a water hose. I still do it as adult, but when we got there, the hose was half rotten and sitting in mud with gnats and flies flying around it. She turned on the water, shook as much of the mud and bugs off of it as she could, and held up the moldy dank hose to her mouth. I knocked it out of her hand.

"Sorry, Peggy, but don't drink that," I said carefully.

"Why not?" she asked. "I do all the time," she protested. I could feel tension building so I spoke as gently and as loving as I could.

"It's not good for you. It's dirty water. Dirty water is never good," I said. "Let's go inside and get a drink." There was some hesitation, as if she was told that we weren't allowed to be inside, but we went in anyway. There was old rickety furniture sitting in odd positions all over the space that I could only assume was supposed to be a living room. The floor creaked with every step we took. There was a wood burning stove in the living room that looked like it hadn't been used in a hundred years, and I didn't see a TV. A very old and heavily framed painting of a man standing in front of a plantation mansion hung awkwardly on one of the walls. My stomach turned a little. We walked straight into the kitchen, where Peggy got two glasses from a cabinet. She started filling them with water from the sink when I turned the knob to what I assumed was the bathroom.

"Don't go in there!" she snapped, almost dropping the glasses. I jerked my hand back like it was a hot cast iron skillet.

"Why?" I asked, eyes wide open.

"We don't go in there. That room is broken," she said.

"What does *that* mean?" I asked.

"The roof fell in when I was a baby, so we don't go in there anymore," she said. I just wanted to cry. I wanted to go home and bring her with me. I wanted to give her new clothes, play in the grass, and eat ham hock pancit out of clean bowls with her. I didn't see her parents anywhere and they never checked on us. That was it. I was calling my daddy.

"Can I use your phone? I want to call my dad," I said.

"We don't have one," she said. At this point I wanted to be mad, but I couldn't figure out whom to be mad at. Peggy drank a full glass of water like she had never had a drink of water in her life. I put my lips to the glass and to pretend to drink and I sat the glass back down. I never went to the bathroom.

The last thing I remember was Peggy sitting on the ground with a spoon eating dirt by the spoonful. "Do you want some?" she asked. Was this a dare, or a meal? I couldn't tell. It didn't matter to me, either way.

"Peggy, I don't eat dirt," I said standing above her. She looked up at me with a certain look in her eyes that could only mean we were going to push our friendship aside and have words. She stood up and threw her spoon down.

"I knew it! My parents were right! I told them you were different, but they told me! They told me you would be stuck up! They told me you would think you were better than me! They were right about you! You think you're better than me?" she asked, getting closer and closer to my face. I kept my feet still, just like when the bus was coming for me on the first day of school.

"I don't think I'm better than you, Peggy, but I don't eat dirt!" I said, like it was an obvious thought.

"No, you're stuck up! You probably live in a real house, with a real yard, and your parents probably cook and put you to bed and stuff! Well, we're free! We don't have to worry about all the stuff like you have to because of money! We can do what we want!" She was clearly regurgitating the rhetoric that her parents tried so hard to brainwash her with, and it had obviously managed to both succeed and fail on some level. She was screaming at me in my face, like she was about to hit me, so I did the only thing I knew to do: I grabbed her and hugged her so hard that we fell to the ground. Then I sat up as quickly as I could, like an expert wrestler trying to control the match. I grabbed her from behind her back and around her stomach and I squeezed as hard as I could while she was crying and struggling to get free. I strained to hold her close to me and keep her still. I closed my eyes and grunted. I thought my arms would fall off, but I didn't let go. After a more than respectable amount of time, she finally gave up. Her body relaxed and she wasn't pushing me away anymore. We sat in the dirt together, both crying while I rocked her back and forth like one of my dolls at home, and I brushed her hair with my hand. I don't know how long we were there. It was long enough for the birds to stop singing. I looked down at Peggy in my arms. Her eyes were shut, and she was crying and shaking, as she let me rock her. Mud was dribbling out of the corners of her mouth. I figured my dad would be coming to pick me up soon. I had a real desire to care for her the best way that I could until it was time for me to leave. While we were still on the ground I said, "You need to brush your teeth, okay?"

"I don't have a toothbrush," she whispered in shame back to me. I started to cry but I held back the tears.

"It's okay," I replied and started rocking her again. I looked over to the house. I saw that her dad had inched a curtain away from the window to watch us. I knew when I looked at him that he had been watching us the whole time. At first, I got really creeped out, but then a surge of bravery rushed over me and I felt like I was standing seven feet tall. It made me feel big. It made me feel strong. It made me assess the situation clearly. I knew who to be mad at now. Instead of looking away, pretending to not see him, I dropped my chin and looked her dad in the eyes fearlessly, like he was nothing less than the devil (with no teeth I might add) and I rocked Peggy and patted her with even more intention, as if she was my puppy and I'd kill anyone who came close. He quickly snapped the curtain shut, and that's when I knew...I knew that I was going to do something.

I went home and weighed out all of the options and I settled on one. I didn't know if it was the right choice, but it was the best that I could come up with. I got on the bus that day with a mission. Those high school girls saw it in my eyes. If they had tried anything with me that morning, I would have pulled a piece of their crunchy hair so hard that it would have probably snapped right off. They left me alone. I walked into school and marched straight into the principal's office, electric paddle or not. I was about to do something I had never done before. I was about to tell... I was about to tell *on adults*.

An assistant lady came into the office and sat down and asked me what I wanted. I told her that I needed to get some parents in trouble. She lifted her eyebrows. I told her everything. I told her about the moldy garden hose Peggy had to drink out of all the time. I told her about the part of the house being caved in. I told her that Peggy didn't have a tooth brush and that she ate dirt, and when I finished my story I asked her very seriously, "What are you going to do about it?"

The look on her face told me she might know more to the story.

"We'll look into it," she said. I believed her.

I went to class and Peggy acted like she didn't know me. She never spoke to me again. She acted like I had never been to her house, and like we had never played on the playground. About a month later, Peggy didn't show up to school. The teacher told us that she moved to Indiana to live with her aunt. She smiled when she told us, and I could have sworn she purposely looked at me several times when she was talking. I had terrible mixed emotions. They were too heavy and confusing for a ten year old to sort through. They kept me up at night every now and then for the next few weeks.

As an adult, I found Peggy on Facebook. I didn't friend request her. I figured if she wanted to be friends with me, I was easy to find. I didn't know if she was embarrassed or maybe she had blocked that part of her life out of her mind completely. Just to let you know, according to Facebook, she is a nurse now. She is extremely beautiful and has a husband and two boys. Oh, and her name isn't Peggy. I changed it for the book. At any rate, if you're reading this Peggy (you know who you really are), please find me. I'd still love to be your friend. We can sit at a park in the cool green grass and you can tell me what you've been doing all these years. Wouldn't it be great if there was a clean water fountain nearby that we could take turns drinking from? You can go first.

Grilled Teriyaki Corn on the Cob

YIELD: 4-6 long ears of corn

- ¼ cup soy sauce
- 1 Tbs. honey
- 1 Tbs. apple cider vinegar
- 1 Tbs. brown sugar
- 1 clove minced garlic
- 4-6 ears of fresh corn, husked

Mix the first 5 ingredients together in a medium bowl for the marinade. Tear pieces of foil large enough to wrap each ear. Brush each ear with the marinade. Wrap the foil around each ear, taking care to seal the edges. Grill 20-25 minutes over medium coals, turning often. Remove from grill. Let rest for 10 minutes before serving.

ASSEMBLY & EATING:

Unwrap the corn from the foil. Slather it with butter and black pepper. Pick up a piece of corn on each end. Hold it up to your mouth. Smell it. Smile. Smell it again. Now take a delicious bite. Say "Mmm." Chew, and while you're chewing and thinking about how wonderfully salty, sweet, smoky and buttery this corn is, take just a fraction of a second to be thankful that you brushed your teeth when you were little and that you're still brushing your teeth today. That's right. Be thankful for your teeth. Take another bite. Those teeth sure are coming in handy, aren't they? Take another bite. My goodness! Isn't it just great that you don't have to gnaw on this corn with your gums? Take another bite, and when you have finished eating your delicious corn, go and do the smart thing. Brush your teeth. You don't want any renegade kernels stuck anywhere. And floss! And if there are kids around you, remind them how important it is that they brush their teeth too. After all, you *do* want to eat corn on the cob for many years to come, right? Of course you do. Especially now, since you have this recipe.

CHAPTER SEVEN

THE GARDEN SONG

Not a pool, not a playground, not a place for play

Only a garden will grow here today

No moss nor meat, only plants to eat

And they grow grow grow, grow 10, 20 feet

The bulbs, the vine, tomatoes held with twine

The squash, the greens, the watermelon dreams

The stones, the stash, potatoes for the hash

The dig, the dig, the shovel, the rig

The corn, the stalk, the daily check walk

The grind, the time, work and unwind

Sprinkler, drinkler, shiny peach twinkler

Put your hands in the fertilizer stinker

Gather, gather, soap your hands lather

The wash, the worms, the garlic confirms

The cut, the chop, the long lettuce flop

The dress, the glass, the once dirty woman

Now a lady with class

The fork, the bite, next bite invite

The swallow, the down, you're inside me now.

Back to the garden, to the garden I go.

Back to the garden, to the garden I go.

Back to the garden, to the garden I go.

Back to the garden, to the garden I go.

THE MIRACLE GARDEN

I had an escape from the woes of the world. It was about a fourth of an acre in size. It was my father's garden. There would be a time in spring when he would start to look out of the heavy sliding glass back door and into the back yard. He would be holding his heavy plastic gas station mug that had a thick handle that we referred to as "his glass." It was massive. It held a liter of drink plus ice, and when you're talking about Danny Haskins, the drink is always sweet tea. He would walk away, and then ten minutes later he would walk back, take a drink, and then silently stare again at the back yard. Sometimes he'd make a comment like, "Still not warm enough," out loud to himself in slight disappointment, talking about the weather.

Weather, soil and seeds- it all came down to weather, soil and seeds. You can have the best weather, but if you don't have good soil and seeds, you don't have a garden. You can have the most nutritious soil on the earth, but if you don't have anything to plant, it's useless. You can have the best seeds that plants can render, but if your soil isn't good, forget it. You're wasting your time. My father always took care to be in tune with the weather, as if many parts of his life were affected by it, not just the garden. When the day came that the weather was behaving the way he wanted it to, he'd make his move on his plan to prepare the garden. He would till almost our entire backyard, by himself, breaking up the dormant winter ground with the tiller- a machine so loud and evil-looking that still, to this day, I have never put my hands on it. He would spend all day out there, coming in only to get more tea. Now that I think about it, my mom, sister and I should have taken shifts to make sure he always had plenty. After all, this garden would feed us all year. Even after the last blackberry bush gave off its last blackberry in the fall, Mom would have already canned many of the vegetables to easily carry us through the winter.

This garden was a miracle place to me. I once thought I heard a voice in the wind telling me that one day I would move to California, to which I looked up and thought I saw my future, but on most days I just spent time with the plants. I wanted to look every seed in the eye before it went into the ground. They needed to understand that I knew what they looked like in seed form and that they had a responsibility to be big, beautiful and plentiful as an adult plant.

"I'm going to remember what you looked like as a seed. Don't be a slacker. See you later," I'd say using my index finger to push it into the dark, soft nutrient-rich soil my father had so carefully balanced. Seed by seed. Row by row. First the radishes and onions, then the tomatoes. The potatoes and corn came after that. Then the melon and squash vines that would eventually grow to have beautiful lily pad-like leaves.

While I was in the garden, I was nowhere else. I wasn't thinking about school, or the mean girls on the bus. I was working on the plants, wondering about the weather, thinking about soil and seeds. I was clumsily dragging the garden hose that had a sprinkler attached to it to the middle of the garden, trying not to trip. I was hoping slimy worms didn't somehow make it into my long black hair. I was wondering how much soap it would take to turn my black hands, which had been impacted with dirt for hours, back to the real color- if that was even possible.

Every now and then, I could hear ice rattle at the bottom of my dad's glass from all the way across the garden. Without looking I knew that meant he had turned the bottom of his glass as far up to the sky as he could, trying to get the last drop of ice cold relieving drink. I knew what was coming. I smiled and waited, like a sprinter at the starting line waiting for the gun.

"Sweetheart!" he would yell across the garden to

me. "Go get me some more tea!"

It was game time, and there was an invisible stopwatch. I immediately straightened to a standing position, and ran to my father to take his glass from his hand while he continued to stare at the dirt in the garden that was causing him to contemplate something seriously. I would run to the house, set his glass on the back steps, run over to the water faucet and rinse off my hands as well as I could with plain water. I used all of my strength to open the 2,000 pound sliding glass door, pick up my father's glass, go inside, shut the 2,000 pound sliding glass door, and go to the 70's style maize yellow refrigerator. I opened the door and poured his tea to the place at the top where I knew I could still run with it and not spill a drop. I shut the refrigerator, fought the sliding glass door all over again, and ran back to my dad and handed him his fresh glass of sweet tea... completely out of breath, but trying not to act like it. He'd take his glass without looking at me, take a drink, continue to stare at the same place he was staring before I went inside and say in a serious tone, "I think I need to put some worms here." I turned my body to look at the dirt he was staring at. I looked at it, put one of my hands on my hips, and pressed my lips together while nodding.

"That's a good idea," I said in agreement, having no idea what he could possibly be talking about. Conversations were deep in the garden.

Then I'd walk back to whatever it was I was doing earlier and pick up where I left off. Months... I got to do this for months. All through spring, summer and even through a little of the fall. I had my retreat in the garden, caring for my father's plants in the made-up ways that only a little girl could imagine. I petted the leaves and told them they were much bigger than last week, and let them know how proud I was of them. I threw the stray pebbles and rocks that the wind had blown close to the plants as hard as I could into the nearby corn field, like they were kidnappers trying to infiltrate a preschool. I lifted up the leaves and when I saw a huge tomato or squash that I had never seen before, I gave it 100 meaningless bonus points for its expert ninja growing skills.

I am fortunate that, as I am writing this today, I can say that my father is alive and well, and yes, he is still gardening. Every spring, the beginning of our phone conversations begin with talk about the weather, and when I hear a certain something in his voice, I book a plane ticket just so I'm there to hear the ice rattling in the bottom of his glass while he stands in his garden.

Summer Garden Salad & Soy Sauce Dressing

Yield: 6-8 servings

SALAD:

- 3 yellow squash, cut into large cubes
- 8 red radishes, quartered
- 4 heirloom tomatoes, cut into large chunks
- 4 cucumbers, cut into similar size as the tomatoes
- 3 green onions, white and green parts, sliced into disks
- 2 Tbs. cooking oil
- salt and pepper

Cut the squash and radishes. Heat a skillet to medium high with the oil. Cook the squash and radishes for 3-4 minutes to remove the raw taste. Sprinkle with salt and pepper while in the pan. While this is cooking you can chop your other ingredients. Remove the squash and radishes from the pan and place in the serving bowl. Add the other chopped ingredients to the bowl and toss with your hands, using gentle fingers.

DRESSING:

- 1/4 cup soy sauce
- 1/4 cup lemon
- 1/4 cup extra virgin olive oil
- 1/4 cup sugar
- 1/2 tsp. garlic powder
- 1/2 tsp. black pepper, or more or less to taste

Put all of ingredients into a mason jar and close the lid tightly. Turn on your favorite tambourine song. Shake while listening. When your song has played for about a minute, your dressing is ready.

ASSEMBLY & EATING:

Pour the dressing on top of the salad in the bowl. Gently fold with a non-metal spoon. Serve immediately. Place the bowl on the buffet table. Try to be third or fourth in line so you don't look so obvious. Talk to someone near you about topics such as school and sports. This will distract people from your genius salad plans that are about to commence, and it will cause people to look at your plate less. When you get to the salad, nonchalantly and almost accidently let the serving spoon pick up most of the radishes. Place them on your plate without looking directly at them while continuing to converse with your clueless accomplice. Only you and Uncle Ron want the radishes anyway... and he's at the back of the line. Take a few steps forward, you're home free. Give yourself a high five on the inside. Yes ma'am. That's right. MAJOR. RADISH. VICTORY.

CHAPTER EIGHT

NO PINOY SNACKS

Pompoms, Yakult, Stik-O, PeeWee

Will not be found in this Walmart I see.

But Lays, Nestle, Hostess and Reese's

are found in bulk and in tiny pieces.

You say, "What's wrong? What is the matter?"

No White Rabbit candy! You can even eat the wrapper!

Ding Dongs here are chocolate cakes?

To me they are peanuts, peas, and corn chip flakes!

I need Prito Rings, Chippy, and Chiz Curlz, please

And don't tell me the last one is missing some "e"s!

Philippine brand Dried Mangoes and Marty's Cracklin's

Make for a meal when you are snackin'.

To get Humpty Dumpty, oh what does it take?

We like to play communion with Haw Haw Flakes.

None of my brands can be found here!

But there are copies, that I did hear!

Boy Bawang is Corn Nuts, and V Cuts are Ruffles,

but calling Clover Chips "Munchos" will get you in trouble.

I'm craving Snacku, Rin-bee, and La La Fish Crackers.

I want Iced Gems too (but only the icing matters).

I must change my tastes, at least Pringles rock.

My only hope for these brands is a balikbayan box.

THE SECRET ASIAN LADY CLUB

We weren't the kind of family that had regular visitors who came to the house during the week, and our weekends were usually reserved for fishing with dad at Reelfoot Lake and grocery shopping (since the nearest grocery store was Walmart, which was about ten miles away). Anytime we had company, we considered it a big deal. We would all get up early and begin working on the house to prepare. My dad would take out the trash and work on the outside of the house, making sure the flowers looked good, and that the driveway was swept. He was also "on call" to drive to the store if my mom had an ingredient emergency while she managed at least four pots on the stove, two pans in the oven, a salad assembly station, and dessert management- which meant she had to constantly protect the cakes from my father's irresistible urge to swipe a taste from the underside when he thought no one was looking. He believed that he was so slick that no one would notice, but we all did because there would be a pronounced divot where his finger or fork made entry, covered by his mediocre attempt of smearing some frosting over it. My mom would seethe with frustration about it the entire time she was cooking.

My sister and I would make beds, polish furniture, and wipe down all the mirrors. Before company arrived, we were required to put on clothes that were "decent" as my mother called it, which meant "better than average." My mom wouldn't be shy about telling us if our wardrobe choice for the day was unacceptable and that we should go "try again." I had learned that this process was less painful and demanding if I could convince a friend to spend the night with me the night before. It was always Michelle, who had funny southern sayings that I had never heard of before and an affection for breakfast fried rice. It was the best of business deals: she kept me entertained and free from polishing furniture, and she got to eat one of her favorite foods.

On this particular day, my mom was having something she called a "Get Together." This meant a group of people were coming over that weren't related to us by blood. This meant that all the Asians she knew in the area were coming over. If it was a big gathering that meant about ten women were coming. Both my mother and father come from large families, so we didn't consider ten people a lot of people at all, but considering that this number could have very well represented one hundred percent of the Asian population across six counties that spanned both Tennessee and Kentucky, this was big. As I recall, the countries represented were: the Philippines, India, Korea, and Taiwan. It was like a middle-aged Asian Miss Universe pageant... with a cooking competition. They began arriving one by one, most of them with their husbands (because none of the women liked to drive, of course), each presenting us with a dish they made. One of my favorite things was to take note of the container with their food in it. Miss Diane, from India, brought her food on a beautiful multicolored plate with a lid that fit perfectly on top. Miss Rachel, also from the Philippines, brought hers in a functional but sturdy plastic container with a tight seal. Miss Kim, from Korea, brought her food in a bowl that was covered with a pattern of red and pink roses with gold inlay. I had never seen so many kinds of food before. It looked way better and far more interesting than any restaurant buffet in the area. The longest green beans I had ever seen in my life were sitting on the table with a dark colored syrupy drizzle on them. I couldn't even imagine where they came from. I had visions of "Jack and the Beanstalk." There was a bowl of soft, green, creamy chunks of something that had bits of onion and fresh ground cracked pepper on top, with a drizzle of glossy olive oil. I would later learn these were called avocados- not a common ingredient in that part of Tennessee at the time. Of course the food that tied all the nations together was rice. Rice gave everyone culinary common ground, and there was no shortage of it. Even though my mother was always an avid sweeper, on party days rice could be found anywhere. Stray grains of uncooked dried rice could be found on the floor in the crack between the cabinet and the linoleum, and my goodness, it hurt if you happened to step on them. Sticky cooked rice would appear in between the presented dishes on the table, probably fallen from people's plates as they came back for seconds or thirds. Sometimes a rogue grain or two would even end up in my hair or on the bathroom floor. I always envisioned those grains as stowaways on a pirate ship (which must have been someone's shoe), trying to escape the mundane and simple life in the kitchen.

After everyone had eaten a plate or two of food, and the women had decided that they all got along well together, the husbands who drove their wives to our house would agree to leave and come back later so the women could spend more time enjoying each other's company without the burden of men. I learned quickly that it was best to go to my bedroom at this time because this is when the women would let their guards down and say things to me like, "Do you know that mole right there on your body? Yes, that one. It means you're beautiful. Oh wait, or does it mean you're clumsy? It might mean you'll never find a husband. I can't remember, but it's okay." This is the kind of thing Michelle's presence would save me from, but unfortunately on this particular day, she wasn't there. They would also start talking really loudly. My mom and her Filipino friends would speak in Tagalog to each other. I never learned the language but I often knew what they were saying, or I could at least get the gist of it. Sometimes I would laugh at the same time they would laugh because I could tell something funny was said, and they would stop laughing to look at me. Then they would have a conversation in Tagalog about whether or not I understood what they were saying. I would interrupt them to assure them that I didn't. Eventually my mom and her friends would encourage me to try to dance or sing like a particular artist for everyone, like Cindy Lauper or Michael Jackson.

"C'mon, Dalena! You a pretty girl! Dance like Michael...ano? Jackson!" they would say in their accent. Then my mom would nod her head to me really hard and point to the floor with her lips. I was a pretty brave girl, but this I simply could not do. I mean, trying to do the moonwalk for the first time in your kitchen for a bunch of Asian ladies that you just met who are clapping at you and pointing with their lips is just is awkward. I had calculated that socks on linoleum were an overall plus for moonwalking, but still, I just couldn't.

I would know if things went well at the party or not based on how my mom would tell me to say goodbye to them. If she said, "Tell Auntie goodbye!" and lingered on the porch with a wave, that meant it went well. If I walked out of my room and I never even knew someone left? That meant I'd never see them again. That rarely happened though. I was really shocked that ten to fifteen Asians existed in the area and found their way to our house, even if they had to come from such a large area in neighboring counties. I remember as a kid thinking that it would be so cool if they had a secret handshake or a pin they could wear on their jackets to signify that they were part of a club that the rest of the town didn't know about. I would pretend that if any of them heard of someone who had suffered an injustice, they could all secretly assemble and do some kind of nunchuck karate on the town's people to avenge their cause, like they all led dual lives: unsuspecting Asian housewife by day, Asian nunchuck superhero by night. But alas, it was not to be. My mom's super powers only manifested in her ability to expand her chicken adobo territory in our fridge. I suspected the same with the other ladies, but they were heroes to me in some way. As an adult, I think about how hard it must have been for these women to live in a place where no one understood their first language, the food of their childhoods, or their cultural traditions. I think it's indeed heroic to be brave enough to take on a life where these things aren't commonly practiced. I'm sure these "Get Togethers" provided a sense of community and familiarity for the women. Certainly there was plenty to bond over as the true and unrecognized minority in the area, no matter which specific Asian country they were from. The "Get Togethers" eventually just fizzled away. My mom remains friends with most of the women, who drop by the house individually whenever they are in her neck of the woods.

Dear all Asian ladies who used to come to my house when I was little, I remember you. Thank you for being kind. You sure did know how to cook the heck out of some Walmart ingredients.

Breakfast Fried Rice aka Michelle's Fried Rice

YIELD: Serves 4 to 6

- 1 pack of bacon, cut into 1 inch pieces
- 4 eggs
- 3 cups cooked rice
- garlic powder, to taste (start with 1/4 tsp.)
- soy sauce to taste (start with 1 Tbs.)
- black pepper, to taste (start with 2 tsp.)

In a frying pan over medium heat, cook the bacon until your preferred doneness. Remove from the pan, leaving enough fat in the skillet to scramble the eggs. Reserve the rest of the fat in a separate bowl.

Scramble the eggs in the same pan. When the eggs are done, add the cooked rice and bacon. Sprinkle in the garlic powder, soy sauce, and black pepper, trying to spread it out evenly. If you want to pour the rest of the bacon fat over the rice, go right ahead. Fold everything together by dragging your utensil across the bottom of the pan and then gently flipping it over until all the ingredients and seasonings are combined well. This method helps keep the scrambled eggs from falling apart too much. Taste and adjust seasonings to your liking.

ASSEMBLY & EATING:

1. Grab a plate before Michelle does, or she'll take most of the bacon and eggs, and she'll say it was an accident. Of course she'll do this right before telling you that she loves you.

2. Serve yourself some rice, leaving plenty of bacon and eggs for Michelle, even though she wouldn't do the same for you. After all, she is a guest in your house.

3. Wait for Michelle to get her plate and her serving, then go into the living room and sit side by side, Indian style, on the carpet in front of the TV.

4. Turn on Saturday morning cartoons with your fancy gray remote control that has a six foot cord which is plugged into the VCR.

5. Eat your breakfast fried rice with your friend. See that Michelle finished hers long before you're done. Remember that there is no more left in the pan in the kitchen.

6. Hold your plate a fourth of the way over Michelle's. Rake half of what you have left onto her plate with your

fork.

7. Speak. "Thank you for coming over, Michelle. I love you."

8. Lean your head to the left and rest it on Michelle's shoulder while you both laugh and take bite after bite of her favorite fried rice, while you watch that crazy coyote and roadrunner try to outwit one another for the millionth time.

CHAPTER NINE

ROCK-A-BYE-REDNECK

Rock-a-bye redneck, in the moonlight,

try to rob our house and we will fight.

Come over here only if you dare,

'cause Uncle Larry will shoot you in his underwear.

SHOTGUNS AND BLACKBERRIES

Blackberries grow wild in northwest Tennessee. It's not uncommon to simply pull the car over on the side of the road and pick them if you happen to see that there are some that have ripened and are being ignored. I was about nine years old when I got to stay at my Aunt's house for a week in Hollow Rock, a town about 60 miles away. The name of the town is directly related to its size and level of entertainment offered there. Aunt Barbie, or "Barb" as we called her, had four little girls about the same age as me and my younger sister. One day when she was "fed up" with our indoor behavior, she handed us all large plastic cups, beaten-up tupperware and riffraff buckets before telling us to not come home until every container was full of blackberries. I told her I had never picked them before.

"It don't matter. The blackberries don't know that," she said and began to laugh. Barb said funny things all the time and there was always a lot of laughing around her.

The six of us wandered down the back roads, singing and laughing and darting in and out of the woods, and looking along the fence lines for wild blackberries to bring home to Barb. We felt like we were gone for hours. We came back home when we were so hungry and thirsty that we couldn't stand to be outside anymore. We got a drink and a snack and were sent back outside because our containers weren't full. This would be considered cruel and dangerous in today's day and age, but it wasn't at all back then. Barbie loved us, but we were told to get a job done, so we had to do it. Not only did we do it without complaining, we really enjoyed it. It gave us an adventure and we bonded at the same time. We never mentioned a concern for snakes, bugs, or strangers, and I don't recall having any to contend with. We just had a really good time getting dirty and sweaty and splashing in the newly discovered creek together. That night we ate blackberry cobbler in the dark on the living room floor, watched "The Goonies" until way past our bedtime, and fell asleep sprawled out all over the living room floor.

In the middle of the night, we heard a very loud and unfamiliar ruckus outside. Living in the country we were used to hearing coyotes and owls. The occasional raccoon might even make its way too close to the garbage outside, but this sound wasn't any of those. It was different. It sounded like people. One by one all of us girls started sitting up in the dark, staying as still and as quiet as we could. We tried as hard as we could to make eye contact with each other in the little moonlight that the small living room window offered. I saw the outline of a man walk past the window at a terrifyingly slow pace. My older cousin, Tanya, stood up and ran to her parents' bedroom. I knew she was going to tell. She was fearless. Being the next oldest, I started to gently feel around for my cousins and sister to give them a relieving pat on the leg even though I was terrified myself. Soon I heard the fast paced heavy footsteps of my Uncle Larry coming down the hall. He was a hunter, and I knew he had to have a stash of guns somewhere in the house. As my eyes followed him in the darkness, I could see that he had no shirt on, and that he was indeed holding one of his shotguns. I could tell by the way he held it that he had history with this gun. He knew every line and curve of it, and he wouldn't have known them any better if the lights had been on. He never looked over in our direction. He walked straight into the kitchen with such determination and heaviness in his footsteps that it made us even more afraid. He didn't turn on the kitchen light. I heard a drawer open hard and slam shut. Soon I could hear the undeniable sound of shells being loaded into a gun and a final click, which I knew meant the gun was loaded. He walked quickly to the back screen door and threw it open so hard I thought he must have broken it. He yelled something in a tone that I didn't know he was capable of speaking in and then fired three shots. Cla-Click, BOOM! Cla-click, BOOM! Cla-click, BOOM! All of the girls started reaching for each other quickly. We didn't dare say a word or cry a tear as we waited in silence for whatever was going to happen next. After the longest ten seconds of silence we had ever experienced, we heard a truck squeal out of the driveway and down the road. My uncle came into the living room still holding the shotgun, and turned on the lamp, which revealed that he wasn't wearing anything except white, worn out Fruit of the Loom underwear, which had clearly seen better days. Being a man of a particular physique, his belly hung slightly over the front elastic, which was barely functional anymore.

"Y'all alright?" he asked, looking in our eyes intensely. We lifted our eyebrows and nodded vigorously to let him know that we were. Barb, who at some point came to sit with us on the floor, said, "Larry, you didn't have to shoot at 'em!"

"Aw, I didn't. I just scared 'em away." We cut our eyes at each other, not knowing what to make of it. Then, like what just happened was perfectly innocent and normal, my Uncle Larry said, "Alright. Y'all go back to sleep."

He turned off the lamp, then he and Barb walked out of the room. We all laid our heads back on our pillows without talking. Then out of the silence we could hear a very heavy, loud and strong steady stream of water coming from the bathroom and we knew it was Uncle Larry... peeing. Thank God! It broke the tension, and all of us started giggling and covering our mouths, trying to not make any noise, but we couldn't help it. When Uncle Larry gave us a grand finale of a full three-second proud and robust fart, which seemed to musically go higher in pitch the closer it came to the end, and finished with the sound of a mouse squeak abruptly cut off by a conductor, we completely lost our senses and any composure we had left in us. We laughed so hard we could take full drinks of our tears if it wasn't for us wiping them away. Barb came out of the bedroom just to watch us try to hold ourselves together. Then Uncle Larry emerged from the bathroom with a smile and said, "Okay, that's enough. Y'all go to sleep." And we did. And we slept like well-kept babies until morning.

Blackberry Moonshine BBQ Sauce

Yield: 5-6 cups

- 4 Tbsp. Minced Shallots
- 3/4 cup Red Wine Vinegar
- 2 cups Worcestershire Sauce
- 1¾ cup Ketchup
- 1 cup Blackberry Moonshine or 1 cup plain moonshine and a handful of blackberries
- 1¼ cup Honey
- 1 Tbsp. Cornstarch Slurry (even parts of cool water and cornstarch, combined well)

Combine all ingredients except the cornstarch slurry. Bring to a boil, then reduce to a simmer for 45 minutes. Add the slurry. Turn the heat back up to medium high and cook for 5 minutes, or until desired thickness. Remove from heat and cool.

ASSEMBLY & EATING:

There is only one thing you really need to do: dip everything you can find in it. Yes, of course it's great on ribs and pulled meat sandwiches, but don't forget the French fries. And wings. Yes, CHICKEN WINGS! Even eggrolls and taquitos, who cares? It's BBQ sauce- it BELONGS on everything. Broiled catfish and fried shrimp too. Everything. Just put it on everything, and look people right in the in the eyes as you lick your fingers while they stare at you like the uncivilized finger-lickin', bad-to-the-bone bar-b-que eating, Carl's Jr./Hardee's commercial model that you are. By the way, you're even cooler than that. They don't know why? Say it loud and proud, "There's moonshine in it!"

CHAPTER TEN

DATURA

You smoked the Datura?

Did it make a fog?

Did you feel proud on your horse in Kingdom bog?

You drank the Datura?

How long did it steep?

Did you chant loudly enough to make your captives weep?

You snorted the Datura? Did it make a mess?

Did you believe you were with God 'cause a cross was on your chest?

You know nothing of Datura. Your sinfulness reeks.

Confederate Jasmine can't cover up your stink.

The white corolla of the Datura makes her move at night,

same as your henchman who play "white robed knight."

You tied and slashed your brother man to prove that you were bold?

I think you all are golden shrimp, without any of the gold.

Is the photophobia the reason you can only come out at night?

No psychotropic antidote, or analgesic light?

Datura whispered to me the thing he'll say to you,

if you don't learn to take Datura for all that is true.

He'll say, "I never knew you. Away from me, be gone!"

Then Datura will drive you down to the place where you belong.

Come clean with Datura, the only righteous One.

Until then the Kingdom trees will sing of what you've done.

KINGDOM

I always enjoyed fishing with my dad. I saw it as a wonderful opportunity to escape from the heavy burdens of childhood. On this particular day, we were going to a fishing spot not very far from our house that he and many other people referred to as "Kingdom." We drove on backroads the entire way there. It was always a bit of a creepy drive, even during the day. The road would get narrower and narrower the closer we got, and the trees and bushes became more and more overgrown. We often saw one or two snakes in the middle of the road that we would just drive over on the way there. Once we got to what seemed like almost a dead end on a barely paved road, we had to roll up our windows because the buzzing from the overpopulated insects would be so loud that it seemed like they were all sitting on our shoulders at the same time, screaming as loudly as they could into our ears. The bugs were so much bigger and braver out there than anywhere else I had ever been. It seemed like they were all old granddaddy bugs- no mommas or daddies or babies. All the bugs were big, mean, old granddaddy bugs...they probably grew their own tobacco, rolled their own cigarettes and smoked them when humans weren't looking. I helped my dad launch his beat-up army green boat into the water, and I began baiting our fishing poles with worms that he harvested from our yard after a rain. Many times we had the watershed all to ourselves. I would fish for my favorite kind of fish to eat: crappie - a non-oily, fresh water fish with milky white fillets that are super flaky and mild in taste. I knew how to manage four cane poles at one time, while my dad bass fished with his back to me, using his favorite top water spinner bait. The air was cool and peaceful. The water was still. I could hear an animal walking through the woods past the bank. My dad and I would make eye contact with each other and nod, knowing it was a good size deer. We constantly kept looking in that direction to see if we could get a glance. Every now and then, I'd lift one of the poles to make sure my bait was still on the hook.

Once we got further away from the bank, the vegetation started looking like species all of their own, like they had secretly survived the Jurassic period. Flowers that normally grew in small clusters stood alone as individuals, opening up to the size of my hand. Trees that were trimmed and tamed in town looked like angry overgrown giants that had never shaved a day in their lives. Even the tall grasses looked stubborn, as if running them over with a steam roller wouldn't even cause them to consider laying down. I could feel that this area had a particular flavor of history that I was unfamiliar with, and it felt like it may have been a terrible one. Taking in the environment so attentively on a particular day made me wonder something that had never crossed my mind before.

"Dad, why do they call this place 'Kingdom'?" He reeled in slowly and casted his lure towards the bank again.

"You don't know?" he asked, without looking at me.

"No," I said, wondering why I would.

"They say they used to hang people here," he said.

"What?" I gasped in unbelief. Just then there was violent splash in the water and my father pulled his pole tight over his shoulder forming the signature bend in his rod when he had a big fish to fight. I couldn't wait to ask more questions, so I asked him while he was trying to pull it in. This is a "no-no" in fishing etiquette. All conversations are supposed to cease for the respect of having a fish on the hook. In this particular moment, I didn't care.

"What do you mean they used to hang people!?" I asked loudly, trying to be louder than the fish splashing and my dad grunting. "Who hung who?" I demanded. I was confused. How could I not know that I lived only 6 miles down the road from a place that was named for hanging people? Why wasn't I taught this already? My dad tried to hush me while he used all his muscle to bring the fish in. I could have hushed and sat down. I was the type of kid that knew my place and I would have normally never even spoken, but this information was almost traumatic. In this moment in time, the height of my dad's fight with the fish coincided perfectly with my most frustrated feeling in this discussion. While he pulled as hard as he could, pole up, tip down, I stood up in the boat and shouted, "Why do they call it Kingdom?!" Just then my father's line broke and there was instant silence for a split second. The fish was gone. The only sound was silence before the bugs resumed their buzzing. My father's once strained fishing line now flew delicately in the air, while we were left standing in the boat, staring at each other. He waited for me to speak first. I was the kind of kid who apologized, but not this time.

"Why do they call it Kingdom?" I whispered, almost in tears. I watched his face as his anger turned to heartache.

"Sweetheart, they used to hang blacks here. They put the n-word in front of Kingdom, and that's what they called it."

I was stunned. I sat down almost in a daze. People had been calling me that word off and on since Kindergarten, and just six miles down the road from our house people who were called that were hung. I had never bothered to tell my parents that I had been called that word so often. What could they do? Chase down every mean person I had ever encountered? And tell them what? Not to say it anymore? Who would force them to listen?

My brain started putting the facts together. Fact: there were people I knew who called me the n-word. Fact: I was in the place where people hung people who were called the n-word. The next logical question I had to ask was, "If someone sees me here, will I be hung?" But I didn't ask it out loud. I was too scared and I didn't want my dad to worry. Even though we were the only people there, and even though my dad's back was facing me, I spent the rest of the fishing trip trying to hide by sinking down into the boat as far as I could, while still managing the poles and pulling up a few good sized crappie. No eyes were looking at me, not even my father's, but I didn't want the granddaddy bugs and the tree giants to tell the regulars they had seen me there.

Beer Battered Crappie

Yield: 3-4 servings

- 1 lb. crappie fillets
- 12 ounces beer
- 1½ cups corn flour
- 1 cup all-purpose flour
- 1 tsp. salt
- 1 tsp. paprika
- 1/2 tsp. cayenne pepper
- peanut oil for frying

Empty the beer into a large mixing bowl. Add everything except for the all-purpose flour to the beer and mix thoroughly with a whisk. Refrigerate for at least an hour. In a cast iron skillet, heat at least 2 inches of oil to 375 degrees. Dredge fillets in flour, shaking off the excess, then coat in the beer batter. Fry until golden brown and drain on paper towels or brown paper bag.

ASSEMBLY & EATING:

Hold hands with those sitting at the table with you.

Bow your heads. Bless your meal with a prayer of thanks and gratitude that you have provision for nutrition, the freedom to eat it, and the ability to enjoy it. Consider those who came before you who could not. Consider those in the world right now who *can* not. Look your friends in the eyes and soak up their beauty. Soak up the moment of togetherness. Soak up the moment of warmth and love. Smile. Be grateful. Eat.

CHAPTER ELEVEN

THE STOLEN CHILDRESS CHILD

Marlena went missing on a golden afternoon.

The darkness came to town because we didn't know what to do.

We tied yellow ribbons, knocked on all the doors,

Pointed fingers at each other, then pointed them some more.

Became dumb and dumber, with Tweedle Dee and Tweedle Dum.

Entered the land of sadness for lack of clues, not even one.

I asked the oracle and Caterpillar where to go.

Told them the ancient ones were moving far too slow.

Let's find Marlena! Baby face and baby bones.

Let's find Marlena! Hope she's not too far gone.

We need Alice and the horsemen, the tulips and the Hatter,

An underwater champion, a wise mushroom matter.

Marlena is missing from her very own front yard!

The Knave of Hearts and Bandersnatch are coming to stand guard!

We'll look down the wells, and climb up the ladders!

Bring soldiers to Union City, where their skills really matter.

Marlena is missing! A tongue must confess!

May the guilty be tormented with shame and unrest!

How do you live, knowing the truth that you hide?

You may walk freely, but your freedom is denied.

Confess for your freedom, your freedom inside.

May prison bars sing songs of peace that tell you confessing was right.

I have not forgotten the stolen Childress child.

Until you proclaim the truth, may her justice drive you wild.

Eat me, drink me, grow me, shrink me.

I'll never forget Marlena, the stolen Childress child.

MISSING MARLENA

"Dalenahhhh!" my mom yelled to me out of the sliding back door. "What are you doing?"

"I'm looking for Marlena!" I yelled back from the side of the house where the scary metal box that ran our central air-conditioning was located.

"She's not there!" my mother shouted back.

"How do you know?" I yelled back, looking around the corners of the box, without looking back at her. "Did you look here?"

"No! But she not there! Come inside! Time to help me practice Pledge of Allegiance for citizen test!" she demanded in her accent.

"I can't today, Mom! I have to look for Marlena!" I explained. My mom closed the sliding door, giving up on trying to get me to give up.

Marlena Childress was a four year old girl who was reportedly taken from her front yard in Union City, ten miles away from our house. I was nine years old at the time, and I had never heard of anyone going missing, except for the kids who were on the milk cartons, and none of them were ever from Obion County, or northwest Tennessee for that matter. Things like this didn't happen here. Everyone knew everyone else's business, all of the time. My town was the kind of town where your dad couldn't pump gas at the gas station without you going to school the next day and your friend telling you that her dad saw your dad walking out of the gas station with a moon-pie and RC Cola. There was no privacy. There were no secrets, and therefore it was impossible for anyone to go missing, especially a four year old girl from her front yard.

The entire tri-state area of Northwest Tennessee, and adjacent Kentucky and Missouri, was turned upside down. The story of missing Marlena was all over the school classrooms, playgrounds, the radio stations and TV. There was nowhere you could go without it being mentioned, yet despite all the chaos, an eerie cloud of silence managed to make an appearance in every conversation about her, like an uninvited and unfamiliar stranger. Search parties looked through the woods and by the river, but there was no trace of her. A couple of arrests were made, but they were let go. It seemed like she had just vanished into thin air.

My nine year old self felt desperate to help, so I searched the only place I could: my yard. Maybe I needed to look for her so I could go to bed and lay my head on my pillow, knowing that I did my part. I meandered all over our yard, which was basically a wide open half-acre plot of land that was always clean cut and manicured, with absolutely no place to hide. I walked around alone, like a detective- like Sherlock Holmes, like the Pink Panther. I didn't know what else to do. If someone would have handed me a magnifying glass, I would have used it to check the underside of the rose bush leaves that were in the front yard, and for fingerprints on the mailbox. Why? I don't know, but I would have. It had totally escaped me that I was alone in my yard, looking for a missing girl that was supposedly taken from her yard. It appeared to have escaped everyone else too, because I looked for her uninterrupted. As I meandered and wandered, looking under small rocks and behind skinny trees, I thought about who the best help would be to find her, since no one was able to find her so far. My mind wandered passed human options and delved into the imaginary. If I could just get the characters from *The Neverending Story* or *Alice in Wonderland* to fly out of the sky and land somewhere, *anywhere* nearby, I just knew we could find her. I would tell my teachers we needed to get all the adults from school to meet me in the cornfield behind my house to meet with our recently-arrived magical champions who had special talents for solving problems that humans can't. I would tell my dad to get all of his tire-throwing friends from Goodyear to join us. I would tell my mom to get her nun-chuck fighting Asian lady friends to come too.

Before I knew it, it was almost dark. The lightning bugs were arriving and so were the mosquitos. I had to go inside. I didn't find her, and there was nothing I could do. I couldn't try harder. I couldn't force others to try harder. I had no one to tell on or go to that could help. I had a hard time eating my supper that night. Nothing tasted right because the flavor was overshadowed by my unsuccessful search and rescue venture. Helplessness is the emptiest flavor I've ever tasted.

Pillow Cake

Yield: One 2-layer, 7-inch round cake

CAKE:

- 5 egg whites, lightly beaten with a fork
- 1 whole egg
- 1 cup whole or almond milk
- 2.5 tsp. pure vanilla extract
- 3 cups cake flour
- 2 cups sugar
- 1.5 Tbs. baking powder
- 3/4 tsp. salt
- 1.5 sticks unsalted butter, cold and cut into pieces

Preheat the oven to 350°F. Grease two 7" round cake pans, line with parchment, and lightly dust with flour. Lightly whisk the egg whites, 1 egg, 1/4 cup of milk and the vanilla in a medium bowl. Set aside. Sift the dry ingredients together into a large bowl. Mix the dry ingredients on low in a stand mixer, then add the butter one piece at a time. Add the remaining ¾ cup of milk, and mix on low for 4-5 minutes. Scrape the sides of the bowl and begin to add the egg mixture a little at the time, mixing until light and fluffy, about 4 minutes.

Fold with a rubber spatula a couple of times to ensure the batter at bottom of bowl is incorporated. Pour the batter evenly into the two pans.

Bake about 20-25 minutes or until a cake tester comes out fairly clean. Remove from oven. Let cool for 10 minutes in the pan before releasing onto wire racks to cool completely.

FROSTING:

- 3 sticks unsalted butter, softened and cut into pieces
- 3 cups sifted confectioners' sugar
- 2.5 Tbs. milk
- 2 vanilla beans, scraped, or 1.5 tsp pure vanilla extract
- Pinch of salt
- 1-2 drops red food coloring, or fresh beet juice to turn frosting pink

Whip the butter for 7-8 minutes with an electric mixer until pale & creamy. Add the remaining ingredients except for the food coloring and mix slowly to incorporate before mixing on medium speed for 3-4 minutes. Add food coloring and continue to mix for an additional 3 minutes.

ASSEMBLY & EATING:

After letting the cake layers cool, use a serrated knife to even the tops of the layers. Frost the top of one layer. Place the unfrosted layer on top of it. Now frost the entire cake, and when you've put on too much frosting, put on a little more. Perfection is not needed. Cut a slice for yourself. Go to the couch. Bring a fork. Sit alone. Be thankful. Be deeply grateful. You are here and can choose to impact the world positively. Smile gently. Take a bite. Make a good decision about something. Swallow. Repeat.

CHAPTER TWELVE

FREEDOM

FREEDOM! FREEDOM! FREEDOM!

The recipe is done!

No more riding that yellow bus, and dealing with everyone!

FREEDOM! FREEDOM! FREEDOM!

From the bullies that hit and stare!

I have a truck! I have my God! I can go anywhere!

FREEDOM! FREEDOM! FREEDOM!

How funny it will be,

when those mean girls see the one driving this truck is me!

FREEDOM! FREEDOM! FREEDOM!

From the girls who have no class,

so understand our wave and smile, when the bus we do pass!

DRIVING MISS DELIA

"Ching, Chong, Ching, Chong!" A boy on the bus pulled the outside corners of his eyes as wide as he could and said this tauntingly as my little sister and I walked by to find a seat. "Y'all are Chinese!" he'd say, trying to make fun of us. I was twelve years old, in the seventh grade, and Delia was ten. This mean boy, who went by the name "Boonie," was more of a man than a kid. He was twenty years old... and still in high school... and he rode our bus. His birthday came early in the school year and he had failed his sophomore year. In our school district in 1989, kids from the high school, junior high, and elementary all rode the same bus. I remember every year, on the first day of school, getting on the bus and hoping that Boonie had finally graduated so that he wouldn't be there any longer. I can't tell you how my heart sank when I'd see his face, smiling at me like he was waiting for my sister and I to get on the bus so could he make fun of us. It made me furious to be around such blatant ignorance and cruelty.

"Calling us Chinese isn't an insult, Boonie," I'd say.

"Why don't you go back to THIGH-LAND?" he'd ask and look around to others, trying to encourage them to laugh.

The bus driver, Mr. Johnson, was very nice but he was very old. He was hearing-impaired and he kept his eyes glued to the road so he never seemed to know what was going on behind him. I tried a few times to tell him that the boys weren't letting my sister and I sit anywhere and that they were always pinching our legs and pulling our backpacks off of our backs, but he didn't take it very seriously. There was no use in telling my parents. My dad couldn't take us to school because he still left for work at Goodyear long before school started, and my mom still didn't drive at all. The bus was the only way for us to get to school, so I didn't want my parents to worry about something that they couldn't fix. I could only think of one solution but it was ridiculous. Soon, I didn't care how ridiculous it was. It was an answer- a *real* answer. And I was going to try to make it happen. One day my dad was gardening in the back yard when I was determined to change this situation. I started to tell him what was happening on the bus. I didn't go into specific details, but I told him I couldn't take it anymore and that Delia shouldn't have to endure it either. He responded with the same response he always gives whenever I have a problem. "You got it a lot better than I did when I was your age, so don't worry about it. When I was your age, I had to walk," then he continued hoeing his garden like the conversation was over. My heart sank. This was a real problem and he basically ignored me. "Then we'll walk," I said as I started to walk away. My Dad stopped hoeing and straightened his back. He knew I wasn't being dramatic. "You'd rather you and your sister walk four miles to school one way and back than ride the bus?" he asked. I turned around and looked at him.

"Yes," I said matter-of-factly.

"Is it that bad?" he asked. This question made me mad but I held it in.

"I wouldn't be out here if it wasn't," I said as calmly as I could, still feeling the stings and bruises on my legs from Boonie. My Dad considered it for a moment before speaking.

"Well, I don't want you walking all that way every day. I had to do it growing up and it's harder than you think. What do you suggest?" he asked.

"I know you can't take us because you have to go to work early. Mom can't take us because she can't drive. The only way for us to get there and avoid the bus, and avoid walking, is for me to drive," I said plainly. I knew he was going to have a strong reaction, so I braced for it. I think he repeated my words in his head a couple of times to make sure that he heard me correctly before he spoke.

"Dalena, you're a good girl but you're only twelve years old and Delia is ten. You don't even know *how* to drive!" he barked at me.

"I can learn right now," I said calmly, never looking away. My dad started hoeing again and began laughing under his breath. He waved his hand up in the air at me as if to say, "Get out of here."

I walked away and went to the front of the house to sit on our small doorstep. I knew my he was thinking about my proposal. I stared at his old fishing truck that he kept parked at the house while he was at work. It was just an old beat up white single cab Chevy, with chipped paint, a window that refused to stay on track, and blue cloth interior that smelled like tires and bologna, but it was every bit of salvation to me. I prayed so hard that I felt my hands making fists. After about ten minutes I heard the sound of keys jingling. My dad was walking towards me. I stood up quickly, waiting for the verdict, my heart almost pounding out of my chest. This was the moment that I had been waiting years for. This was the moment that would determine my school bus destiny. My dad very naturally walked over to me. "Come on," he said. I was so excited that I tripped over my own feet while following him across the flat grass to the truck. He gave me a two minute tutorial on how to start it, where the gears were, and which pedals did what. My hands were shaking and I was trying not to cry from joy. "Drive it around the house a couple of times and see how you do." It took me a few tries to get a feel for the gas and brake pedals, but I was soon driving in circles around our eighteen hundred square foot house. Tires and bologna never smelled so good! My mom and sister must have heard the truck driving in an unusual pattern because they had stepped outside to see what in the world my dad was doing. When they saw it was me, their mouths fell open. Then he waived me down to tell me to drive down the road to practice. He didn't want my sister to feel left out so he told me to take her too. All he said was, "Be careful." She got in the truck and we headed down our country road that I can remember being gravel once upon a time. We went about a mile and drove back. I turned back into our driveway and parked where my dad was waiting. I got out and extended my arm like a soldier, handing the keys back to him. He took the keys and looked at me very hard. I remained perfectly still, holding my breath, while he made his decision. "Okay," he said, handing the keys back to me, and so I began driving Miss Delia at age twelve.

Grilled BBQ'd Bologna Sandwich

- Slices of Bologna, depending how many sandwiches you want
- Blackberry Moonshine BBQ Sauce (or whatever BBQ sauce you have handy)
- White Bread
- Your favorite sandwich Condiments & Toppings

ASSEMBLY & EATING:

Remove the red film from around the bologna. Cut four even slits like a cross into the bologna, keeping the center intact. (Bologna tends to curl in when you cook it. The slits will help prevent this.) Throw it on a hot grill, brushing liberally with your favorite BBQ sauce until it is done the way you like it. I prefer to cook it until it looks like the sauce has become a part of the bologna, rather than a condiment sitting on top of it. I like char marks. Make a sandwich with it, adding your favorite sandwich condiments and toppings. My favorites are Miracle Whip, homegrown tomatoes, and iceberg lettuce. Yours might be too. Have the Miracle Whip versus mayonnaise debate with those waiting for their bologna to cook on the grill. By now, you are a pro. Inform them that Miracle Whip is called "salad dressing" by those who know what they are talking about; however, it is never to be put on a green leaf salad. Inform them that you understand these things don't make sense to "outsiders" but to "us" it makes all the sense in the world. Besides, the fact that it is called "salad dressing" (even though it is not to be used on green salads), puts it in a completely different category altogether than mayonnaise, even though they look exactly the same and are neighbors on the same shelf at the store. Explain to them that obviously, a person preferring one over the other comes down to personal taste, but in the end, you use mayonnaise for recipes, but you use Miracle Whip for the memories.

CHAPTER THIRTEEN

PAINT MY POINTE SHOES

I take the brush and mix the paint

while dreaming of the cheers,

to make a shade that is right

and equal to my peers.

I brush the paint on my pink shoes

so they will match my skin.

Too dark, too light, no shade just right

for my feet to dance in.

No I won't cry cause I'll soon fly-

a soaring ballerina!

Sweatshop House, Nutcracker Mouse,

But soon I will be Prima!

No pancake makeup nor tan tint will ever get me down.

With my hard work I will soon take

my Prima encore bow!

AFRO BALLET

The look on my friend's face was awful. With crinkled eyebrows, red hot cheeks, and her eyes shut tightly, her facial expression told the story of her lifting two hundred pounds over her head, but she wasn't. She was sitting on the floor with her legs as far out in the splits as she could get them, with her stomach almost touching the floor, her chin lifted to the ceiling, sweat dripping from her brow, and our ballet instructor sitting on her back… like really sitting. Like sitting as if she was straightening out her skirt after getting into a limousine. Sitting as if she was about to pull out a magazine and read it from cover to cover. Sitting as if she was sipping a cup of tea, about to ring a bell for Jeeves to bring her a crumpet. It was mean. It was torturous. It was normal. It was ballet.

Miss Poppi and I knew we didn't like each other pretty instantly. She was a little over five feet tall and maybe weighed in at a buck ten, soaking wet. She had all these grandiose stories about "almost dancing here" and "almost dancing there" and would lift her eyes up to the ceiling and stare off as if she was traveling away on the wings of her own stare. Every week she would comment on the weight of every single dancer, giving warm long hugs to the ones who looked like they had nothing more than skin on top of their bones, while acting as if the rest of us weren't even in the room.

Like her, I was about five feet tall and little over hundred pounds, but I was only eleven years old with developed muscles from working in the garden, helping my dad pull his boat, and occasionally playing basketball. At this stage in my life, I was taller than everyone else in my class, and my body had developed more quickly than other girls my age, but I never thought of myself as fat or overweight, and neither did anyone else, as far as I knew. But to Miss Poppi, I was a full-blown obesity case. "See? A little fat roll here. And still so young," she'd say while shaking her head and pinching my side, as if I was a lost cause. Then of course, there was the issue of my skin color. "You look like a zebra in your light pink leotard and tights," she'd say as if she was facing a problem that had no answer. "Everyone else's skin blends in. See?" she'd say pointing to the other girls in class, while trying to stage a scene in our upcoming production of *The Nutcracker*. "I don't know where to put you because you break up the continuity. Maybe you just need to be a mouse," she'd say with an air of catastrophic concern, as if our community ballet production in Union City, Tennessee, was the equivalent to the Bolshoi Ballet in Moscow. I knew I was better than a mouse. Even though I was larger than the other girls in class, I was the most flexible and I had a lot of natural talent. I could do the splits before my first ballet lesson. I had a natural turn-out and an arched pointe that was bent like a "c" curve without even trying. My middle fingers gracefully fell towards my thumbs without her having to tell me, and my jetés were so strong, it sounded like matches being struck on a matchbox. I even instinctively knew that when a position hurt, my face was supposed to be as gentle as a swan. All of these things, I just somehow knew… and she hated it.

She sat on my friend's back who was trembling beneath her, as she gazed over the rest of the class, all doing their best splits, to see who would be her next sitting stool. We had been holding our positions for what seemed like forever. Even the air felt like it was under pressure to please her. Small squeaks, deep inhales and loud exhales were the evidence of the class's discomfort, but not mine. I thought I could take a nap. The most difficult part of it for me was keeping my chin up, but I managed. I lay in the splits with my stomach and chest so heavy on the floor beneath me that I was practically melted into it. My legs and toes didn't just point perfectly out to the left and right, they were beginning to pull even further back, towards the wall behind me. All of this was just fine with me. In fact, you could've given me a piece of gum and a TV and it would have made for a great afternoon.

"Try to get your chest to the floor, and point your toes!" she exclaimed. "Relax your muscles and melt into the floor beneath you!"

I wanted to yell back at her, "I'm not just melting into the floor, lady. I AM the floor!" She should've complimented me, but I knew she wouldn't. Sometimes she would look at me as if to ask, "How in the world are you doing that?" And I would want to say back, "Yep, fat zebra roll and all."

This dynamic between us was bearable until the day I came to class with a very in-style spiral perm. I had always wanted hair like in the MTV videos and Bop magazine. My mom had taken me to Fantastic Sam's for a perm. Four bottles of that formaldehyde-esque perm solution later and I had ringlets that were so twisty and tight it shortened my overall hair length by at least four inches... and I loved it. I loved it so much. It was the best hair that was ever on a head, and it was on MY head. I was going to conquer the world with my hair and my Rave hairspray. At least that's what I

128

thought until I went to ballet class for the first time after having it done. Miss Poppi couldn't bite her tongue anymore. "Girl, you got that nigga' hair now," she said in front of the entire class and then laughed out loud. As I was walking to the bathroom after class, a girl who had always been perfectly polite to me in the past stopped me in the hallway and said, "We don't do afro ballet here," before turning up her nose and walking past me. When Miss Poppi made that statement to the class, she gave them all permission to treat me differently, and a few of them did.

I got in my dad's truck after class. I was quiet. I was trying to figure out how to quit ballet without telling him what exactly had happened. He eventually got the story out of me, but I had intended on not saying a word. I'm not sure why I was trying to handle it that way, but I did. When I repeated the words that were said to me that day, my dad instantly turned the car around and started driving back towards the studio. He instructed me to get out of the car and to go inside with him. I was scared. I had never seen a man inside the building before. It was a place for moms and daughters. I knew when we walked in that people would stop dead in their tracks, and they did. When we opened the heavy door which lead to the lobby, Miss Poppi was standing there with her favorite group of students and their mothers, laughing and giggling. When their eyes saw my dad standing in the door with me behind him, the look of terror fell across all of their faces and they all turned white as ghosts. I was told to wait in the lobby. I don't know what words were said between the two of them in her office while I sat there in the eerily quiet lobby, but when they came out, Miss Poppi was fighting back tears and my dad was holding a check. It was a refund check for the payments he had made for future classes. I wasn't going to be coming back, and I didn't mind.

Sometimes I wonder what could have happened if I had a different instructor in a larger city where maybe minds were more open and there were more opportunities for dancers. It is a shame that there are places in the world that don't have many opportunities in the arts. I wonder how many people have gone their entire lives with undiscovered God-given talent. It crosses my mind that the best actors and actresses, singers, artists, dancers and writers have lived and died without the world ever being introduced to them. I hope there is a big stage in Heaven where the talent that God placed in them is properly acknowledged and put to good use. As for me with all of my unused natural ballet talent, I forgave Miss Poppi a long time ago. Her statement was based on her personal experience and knowledge, neither of these things do I have a right to judge, and I like to believe that she learned her lesson and ultimately became a better teacher for it. And my hope is that those of you who are reading this will learn a lesson too: to either be more aware of the words you use in the world, and to forgive the people who don't.

Big Ballerina's Blackened Pork Chops

Yield: 4 chops

- 4 Pork Chops (about 1/2 pound each)
- 4 Tbs. Butter
- ¼ tsp. Cayenne Pepper
- ½ tsp. Thyme Leaves
- ½ tsp. Oregano Leaves
- 1 Tbs. Paprika
- 1.5 tsp. Cumin
- 1.5 tsp. Garlic Powder
- 1.5 tsp. Onion Powder
- 2 tsp. Black Pepper
- 2 tsp. Salt
- Bacon grease, enough to cover the bottom of your frying pan, about ¼ inch deep

Make a dredging station with 2 bowls or dishes, large enough for one chop to fit in completely. Melt the butter in the first dish. Mix the spices together in the second dish. Heat the bacon grease in a large skillet over medium- medium high heat. Working with one chop at a time, coat both sides of the in butter, then in the spices. Fry for 3-5 minutes each side. Try not to fuss with them while they are cooking. This could cause the spices to fall off. Turn and cook on the other side, until done to your liking. Let rest on a brown paper bag or paper towels for 3 minutes before serving.

ASSEMBLY & EATING:

When you are finished eating, go to your bedroom and lock the door. Make sure the blinds are drawn. You are full from eating Big Ballerina's Blackened Pork Chops, darlin'. This is NO time for jeans. Unsnap those suckers and pull 'em down! Take a deep breath and make a relieving sound on the exhale. "AHHH!" Turn profile in your full length mirror and lift up your shirt and let your belly hang out. C'mon, you don't always do it, and there's nothing wrong with giving your belly a loving "steering wheel around the world" pat in the privacy of your home, like those local men do so shamelessly while walking out of that really good Mexican restaurant in town. Oh, your shirt is in the way? Take it off! Why not? You're alone. Be free and unashamed! Try to do that Russian squat dance thing, but don't hurt yourself. Yes honey... I know you only have on your underwear and you're full of pork chops.

It's okay to laugh at yourself. C'mon! Let loose! Be free! Let that jiggle wiggle, baby! It's okay. Really, it's okay. Your manners will be waiting for you tomorrow when you restart your diet, and so will your sit-ups.

CHAPTER FOURTEEN

CATCHING A BREAK

Oh the joy of catching a break!

I can jump!

I can dance!

I can look instead of glance!

All for the joy of catching a break!

Oh the relief of catching a break!

I can breathe!

I can stand!

I can hug my fellow man!

All for the relief of catching a break!

Oh the peace of catching a break!

I can nap!

I can sleep!

I have no reason to weep!

All for the peace of catching a break!

CLOSE ENCOUNTERS OF THE POLICE KIND

I had been driving for about 3 months into my seventh grade junior high school year. I had established a very smart system of taking backroads all the way there and parking in the back of the school by the gym. My sister knew our system of sneaking in through the back doors by the gym locker room. The teachers all parked in the front or on the side, so no one ever really saw the truck there all day. We would linger around after school waiting for most people to leave, killing time by doing homework or playing basketball. I wrote poetry in my journal that my basketball coach, Carol Little, gave me to encourage my writing. When the coast was clear, we would exit through our trusty back gym door, hop in the truck and head home. On one particular day, my basketball practice got cancelled, and my sister decided to go home with a friend, which gave me an opportunity to drive home alone. I looked forward to experiencing the seven minute drive all by myself and savoring complete freedom and independence, as if I were a grown woman. As I turned the truck around to exit the parking lot, I could see a patch of black shiny liquid on the ground where my truck was parked. I put the truck in park, got out and went over to inspect it. I didn't know much about the inner workings of a truck, but I knew I was looking at oil. I remember thinking that maybe some of the 11 million gallons of crude oil that Exxon Valdez spilled in Alaska made its way to Tennessee through some underground means. My 12 year old mind would rather it had been that than for my dad's truck to need a repair of some kind. I started driving home with a heavy heart, preparing to deliver the news of an oil leak to my father, unable to relish my solitude with a loud and overly dramatic rendition of "Raspberry Beret" by Prince that I had planned during fifth period, when suddenly I saw flickering blue lights dancing across the dashboard. Could this be an angel sent to rescue me from having to see the look on my father's face as he would undoubtedly and immediately calculate the potential cost of a mechanic when I would soon tell him about the oil I discovered? No. No, it wasn't an angel of any kind. In my rear view mirror was nothing short of a horror. A police car with flashing blue lights was behind me with a very official looking man inside. I was barely taught how to drive, and I certainly wasn't taught what to do if there was a cop car following me with its lights on. I needed time to think and weigh out my options, so I decided to drive around a while. While driving, I reasoned that going home and having the cop pull into the driveway with me was the worst thing to do, so I scratched that option off of my virtual list. My next option was to hit the gas and try to get home and go inside before the cop could get me, because surely if I made it into the house and closed the door, that would mean he lost. My dad's truck wasn't very fast though, and the engine had a tendency to die when I made a sharp left turn. I concluded that outrunning the cop was not a good option. I decided I should just stop driving. And so I did- in the middle of the road. A police officer got out of the car and began walking up to my window. I quickly made sure the window was on track and I rolled it down.

"Why did you stop in the middle of the road?" he asked.

"Because I don't want you to go home with me," I responded.

Looking at the man, I realized I knew him. His son was in my grade and had a crush on me two years ago, in Miss Deanna's class. I could tell by the look on his face that he recognized me too. At some point I had drawn the conclusion that I was going to be known whether I liked it or not because of my skin color. I decided that if I was going to be known anyway, I should be known for something *other* than my skin color, so I became very active in school and in the community. Although I no longer took ballet, I played softball and basketball, and I was in every club I could join at school. Because people buy newspapers when kids are in it, the Union City Daily Messenger covered a lot of kid stories, and because I was so involved, I was in many of them. I was officially exiting the phase of being known for my skin color, and I was entering a phase where I was known for being a good reliable kid who worked hard, but at the moment, I was a good reliable kid, who was pulled over by a police officer because I was illegally driving a truck.

"Do you know I've been following you for three miles?" he asked.

"Yes," I said, wondering why he would ask that. Every time I spoke, he seemed to get more confused.

"You're that Haskins girl, aren't you?" he asked, calling me by my last name.

"Yes," I replied.

"You're in my son's class. What are you doing driving?" he asked, trying to piece the puzzle together.

"Going home," I said. The answers to all of his

questions seemed very obvious to me, but I was careful to remain respectful. There was a long pause.

"From where?" he asked, growing more frustrated.

"School," I said. How could he not know that? His son was in my class. He should know what time school gets out.

"Haskins, you're in the seventh grade. What in the world are you doing driving home from school?" he asked sternly.

"Well, I drove there this morning, so I have to drive back," I said plainly. He calmed his frustrations before speaking to me again. He spoke calmly and slowly.

"Haskins, you're 12 years old. Why are you driving in the first place?" he asked.

"The bus is a bad place for me and my sister so we can't ride it. My dad leaves for work long before we have to be at school. My mom doesn't drive. My parents won't let us walk because it's too far. If we're going to go to school, I have to drive us." Then I looked him in the eyes and waited. He thought for a very long time. He thought for so long I couldn't imagine what he had to take into consideration. I thought this talk should go much faster. After all, we were parked in the middle of the road.

"So, your parents *know* you're driving this truck?" he asked.

"I hope so. My dad told me to. I don't think he'd like it if I let someone else drive," I said. He breathed sharped air out of his nose, almost laughing in disbelief. "Mr. Smith?" I asked.

"Yes?" he said.

"Why'd you pull me over? I know I wasn't speeding."

"Because I saw your dad's truck out on the road and I knew Goodyear hadn't let out yet and that your momma doesn't drive, so I was worried about who might have his truck," he said soberly. "You really can't go to school unless you drive?" he asked in confused astonishment.

"No, sir," I said.

"Your folks ain't got no people around, do they?" he asked, meaning they didn't have any family around. I thought about that for a minute.

"No, sir, not close by," I said. He thought hard and then took a deep breath.

"All right," he said, tapping the place on the door where the window comes out (I was actually afraid he might knock it off track, but I didn't say anything).

"This is a special set of circumstances. If I'm going to give you special treatment you can't tell anybody about this. I mean nobody, you got it?" He said it to me so mean, I thought he was mad at me, but it was still music to my ears.

"No, sir!" I said enthusiastically.

"And don't you ever speed or pass anybody on the road. Don't you ever let me catch you on 51 either," he said pointing at me, referencing the highway. "Nobody, I mean nobody! You can't tell a soul."

"I promise," I said.

"Just don't let me see you, ok? If you see me, you turn this thing around and go a different way."

"Okay, okay. Thank you, Mr. Smith!" I said gleefully.

I drove the rest of the way home so thankful that all I had to do was tell my dad about an oil leak. He didn't even think it was a big deal.

That night after supper I went to bed early. I must have thanked Jesus a million times that I wasn't being sent off to prison with all the murderers and bank robbers. I never even saw little girls in prison on TV or in the movies, so that meant I could have been the first one ever. Oh, the shame that I would have brought on my family! I made a decision to never get into that kind of trouble again.

A few months later, my mom got her driver's license and starting taking my sister and me to school. Every now and then, my mom would be driving us somewhere in town and I would see Mr. Smith sitting in his police car. I would always smile and wave as big as I could, even if he never smiled or waved back. I thought he would be so happy to see that I wasn't driving. My mom and sister grew to dread us seeing his car because they thought I was making such a fool of myself to the local police. They didn't understand that he and I had history. Then finally, there was one time when I smiled and waved to him as big as I could, and wouldn't you know it? With two hands on the steering wheel, and without moving a muscle on his face, he lifted one of his index fingers just ever so slightly, and I knew it meant he was waving "hi" back. I responded appropriately- by cheering inside of our car, like my favorite team had just won the Super Bowl. For the record, the name of the police officer was not "Mr. Smith." And for the record, this entire story may or may not have happened. Only me and "Mr. Smith" really know, and we're not telling anybody.

Hot Chocolate Rocky Road Popcorn

- 1 bag (3 ounces) microwave popcorn (preferably with less butter and salt)
- 1/2 cup salted cashews or peanuts
- 1/2 cup miniature marshmallows
- 1/2 cup semisweet chocolate chips
- 1 tsp. butter or shortening
- a few dashes ground cayenne pepper (optional)

Pop the bag of popcorn and pour it onto a baking sheet lined with parchment paper. Discard any unpopped kernels. Sprinkle the nuts and marshmallows over top. Gently move everything around with your hands if you want to incorporate it more. In a microwave-safe bowl, microwave butter, chocolate chips, and cayenne pepper. stirring every 15 seconds. When the chocolate is thoroughly melted, drizzle it over the popcorn mixture. Allow the chocolate to harden (about 10 minutes) before serving.

ASSEMBLY & EATING:

There is a trade secret, kept in the cookbooks of our

foremothers, written by monks in the ancient recipe boxes of the Himalayas, whispered by the storytellers in the lost tribes, known now only by the popcorn makers, brittle bakers and candy shakers that are sprinkled across the earth in pockets of secrecy. Thou must listen closely while I reveal this wisdom to you:

While the chocolate is cooling, a peculiar behavior will start to overtake those nearby. They will find it increasingly difficult to do the simplest of things, which is wait- simply wait. Although they know the dish will be best enjoyed after allowing the chocolate to "set," slowly, one by one, they will chart their courses to the destined cookie sheet, to slip their fingers into the treasure, defiling the intended end presentation with their lack of restraint. There has been only one course of action proven to prevent such an atrocity. Only one proven method: 1) Make sure that you are wearing your full suit of armor that you keep in the coat closet for emergencies- it is required for such a time as this. 2) Do not think that you have no need for your helmet or sword- you do. People are savages, and the mere proximity of a human in the midst of chocolate drizzled popcorn sprinkled with miniature marshmallows and nuts will arouse the most barbaric sugar craving transformation of any mortal. 3) Stand guard bravely in the face of the enemy! They know not what they do! Until the chocolate has cooled, forming a perfect shell on the popcorn and nuts, I tell you, stand guard and hold steady! That is... unless your fingers start to wander into it, then eat some through your helmet. Then fiercely point your sword at those who try to emulate your behavior! (You hypocrite!) However, you *are* the one who made it so it's logical that... Oh, whatever! Those are the rules!

CHAPTER FIFTEEN

SKIRTING THE GRIND

Breaking, escaping, avoiding waking.
We're in it together, skirting the grind.

We bond and we're bonded,
Boredom bound absconded.
Don't be so harsh, man.
You know we're just some kids.

Freedom fingers, wind blowing seekers,
Cigarettes and beepers.
Take it easy, lady.
After all, we're only kids.

Belly laugh chuckle, western belt buckle,
Fist bump fighting knuckles.
It's okay, officer.
We're just being kids.

We're breaking, escaping, avoiding waking.
We're in it together, skirting the grind.

GRAVITY HILL

I spent most of the summer of 1991 worried about what my fate would be in the fall. It was a time when people would take even the ugliest, most rundown car they could get their hands on, lower it as close to the ground as possible, and install thousand dollar bass systems that took up the entire backseat, even if they were unsure if the car's engine was in good enough condition to be considered completely reliable. It was a time when bright tights and jelly bracelets were going out of style, and brown lipstick and tight rolling your jeans was in. Yes, the world was changing in a way that my wardrobe was unprepared for, and to top it all off- I was going to start high school.

I expected there to be drama. After all, it was hard enough for me to overcome questions about where I was from and why I looked the way I did when I started kindergarten. Now I was embarking on a whole new challenge: starting over at the bottom of the totem pole in one of only three high schools in the entire county, the place where four elementary schools converged in a mass transit hallway system of teenage insecurities, hormones and fear. Never did I imagine the gift that life had waiting for me there. It was almost as if God was paying me back for the trouble I endured in my youngest, most vulnerable years of elementary and junior high. Gosh darn, wouldn't you know it? I got to high school and people *liked* me.

I was fortunate enough to have three friends that I never got tired of.

Teresa and I found each other pretty quickly. She had long dark blonde hair, peachy-pink skin, and eyes that changed color back and forth from blue to purple to green depending on what she was wearing. We figured out how to reserve a little of our money each meal at lunch time so at the end of the month we could take a girl trip on our beat-up bikes to the thrift store in town to buy a new shirt or pair of shorts that we would inevitably end up sharing throughout the school year. She had the sweetest sounding bell on her bike- it sounded like dancing baby stars flying out of a glitter baton, about to grant a wish. She would repeatedly and aggressively ring it like a truck driver's horn right before cussing people out that came close to us on the street. RING RING! RING RING! "Watch where you're going, you dumb ass!" I wasn't much of a cusser, but her doing it made me crack up every time. It was like having my own little Tinkerbell… with a potty mouth. She was bubbly, funny, loud, sweet and the only person in my life who could be a little bossy with me and get away with it. I just loved everything about her.

Christy was the girl everyone knew, and she knew everyone. She had olive skin, brown hair, a fondness for macaroni and tomatoes, and was known for telling the truth so blatantly that some people were afraid to be around her. No matter if we were at the gas station, the grocery store or at Blue Bank catfish restaurant on Reelfoot Lake, she knew every single person there. I remember wondering if her family discovered Obion County or if they owned all of it. How else could someone know so many people? I thought about asking her if she was related to Christopher Columbus, and if she was named after him. I refrained.

Jennifer had hair so blonde it almost looked white. Her skin was so pale that she couldn't stay in the sun for ten minutes without being concerned about burning. Her blue eyes made me wonder if God took a piece of the clearest spring day sky and placed it right inside her eyes the day she was born. Jennifer's house was infamous in high school. It was spacious, with a swimming pool and plenty of parking. Her parents were good businesspeople and they were kind. They let large groups of us come over and they genuinely loved us. They would feed us and let us spend the night. It was always good, clean fun there. It was quickly established as the place our core group of friends would meet before going anywhere. Jennifer had cousins in Arizona who had access to music that we in Obion County didn't, and when a large group of us got together, it wouldn't be long before Jennifer busted out a clear TDK tape. We knew what was on it- music that we envisioned all the other kids in bigger cities across the country listening to. When that tape came out, the party was on.

There's a strange place where I'm from that you can go to if you know how to get there, or if you know someone who does, and it's a place that is better to visit at night. Teresa, Christy, Jennifer and I all knew where it was, but as freshman in high school, we needed a way to get there.

We would sit in a circle around the clear landline phone with pink and blue wires at Jennifer's house on a Friday night after school, and Christy would go to work. She would think through the roster of people she knew, dial their number from memory, and within five minutes someone was on their way to "come pick us up and give us a ride." That's right. If Christy was around, you had a 90's version of Uber. The destination? Gravity Hill. The name alone invokes excitement and mystery and the place does not disappoint.

The driver of the night would arrive. It was usually a boy, two years older than us, who had a car, a crush on Christy, and had managed to scrape up some gas money. Jennifer lived so far out in the woods that you could hear cars coming down the road long before it got to the house, and it was just enough time to secure our tight rolls for the eighteenth time that day, and for Jennifer to grab her cassette tape. Before we knew it, we were on our way to Gravity Hill, radio turned up, singing and rapping music that wasn't played on local radio: Paperboy, Wreckx-n-Effect, and Shaggy. If you haven't heard a giddy group of girls with country accents rapping "Ditty" by Paperboy, you're missing something.

The directions to get there are still the same: you go down the road that you're supposed to go down. You turn left. Then you turn right. This is the point where you turn the volume all the way down, and you drive very slowly. The road is as dark as dark chocolate that has been melted in the bottom of a black cast iron skillet. There are no street lights. It's so dark and quiet that it almost feels like you are driving in outer space. I could always feel my eyes instinctively holding themselves open a little wider, desperately trying to see what couldn't be seen in the dark. When you get to the bottom of a certain hill, you put the car in neutral, and you wait. Your car will start slowly rolling backwards...up the hill, like marshmallows that defy gravity when they expand upwards after being placed under heat. It never fails. There was only one way to make this adventure even more potentially perilous: roll all of the car windows down and repeat the process until the fear is so great that someone yells, "I give!" Then everyone rolls up their windows and screams until they laugh.

This was our "something to do." This was our "good time." I thanked God when I got to hang out with these girls and we had a fun carefree night that left our sides hurting from laughter. It was so different from what I had been used to years previously on the bus. I had turned a corner in my life. I was in high school, and I had a posse.

Smoked Chocolate and Whiskey Caramel S'more Dip

Yields: 4-6 serving

(For this recipe I use an 8 inch cast iron skillet.)

CARAMEL:

- 1 cup granulated sugar
- 1/3 cup Scotch whiskey
- 3 Tbs. unsalted butter, softened
- Pinch of salt
- 1.5- 2 Tbs. cream

Cook sugar in a dry 2-quart heavy saucepan over low-medium heat until it begins to melt. Continue to cook, stirring occasionally, until sugar is melted into a deep golden caramel. Remove from heat and slowly stir in Scotch, butter and salt (caramel will steam vigorously and begin to harden). Slowly stir in cream. Cool sauce to warm.

S'MORE DIP:

(ingredient amounts vary depending on your personal preference)

- 1 Tbs. butter
- 1.5 cups smoked chocolate chips, (or a combo of smoked chocolate chips and regular milk chocolate chips)
- 15-20 jumbo marshmallows, cut in half
- Graham cracker squares

Place your oven rack in the center position. Put your cast iron skillet on the rack while your oven is cold, then preheat your oven to 450°F. Once preheated, use an oven mitt to remove the hot skillet from the oven. Swirl the butter in the pan to coat the bottom and sides. Pour the chocolate chips in an even layer into the bottom of the skillet. Arrange the marshmallow halves on top of the chocolate chips, cut side down, covering the chocolate completely. Bake for 5 to 7 minutes, until marshmallows are toasted to your liking. Remove the skillet from the oven and let rest for 3-5 minutes to allow the chocolate to melt more. Drizzle with caramel immediately before serving with graham cracker squares.

ASSEMBLY & EATING:

Cast iron stays hot for a long time. If you are serving this to kids, which you can, because the alcohol cooks out of the caramel, be smart and scoop servings onto individual plates or bowls for them. It's the adults that will give you problems. They will tell you that they want to eat this directly from the pan, instead of using the plates you have offered. You will tell them no. They will persist. Ask them if they would like to pray first. They will ask you why. Tell them it's because they might burn their hand on the skillet. They will say that they won't. Then they will, to which you then graciously keep your mouth shut, smile gently, and offer the plate again without saying, "I told you so." Oh, who am I kidding? You say it. It would be weird and smug if you didn't.

CHAPTER SIXTEEN

THE PIT

The thunder booms and the lightning strikes,

no you're not in a storm, you're at The Pit.

The earth shakes beneath you with all its might,

no it's not an earthquake, you're at The Pit.

Home or visitor? Predator or prey?

Pick your poison, you're at The Pit.

Wave your flag and wave it high,

or sit down and breathe your defeated sigh.

Rebel yell and Rebel cry,

Civil war, eye for an eye

Surrender and run, your prayers unfit.

No, this isn't hell. This is The Pit.

REBEL YELL

Entertainment in Obion County is a subject that doesn't last long in conversations. Other than going to the movies, there has never been much to offer. Our community did have one thing that consistently drew crowds, one thing that always brought what little diversity in colors and nationalities we had in the community together, one thing where there was a chance of getting a glimpse of the people who were providing the entertainment out and about in the community, like seeing a movie star in Hollywood. I'm not talking about musicians or anyone on TV. I'm talking about sports.

Basketball was taken very seriously at Obion County Central High School, or "Central" as we called it. Our mascot was a gray man figure standing in front of the Confederate flag. We were called "The Rebels," and when the Confederate flag was on school grounds, it was called "The Rebel Flag."

On Fridays during basketball season at lunchtime, there were two types of students: the ones who ate lunch in the lunchroom, and the ones who stood in line at the gym in order to buy tickets for their family for the basketball game, which wouldn't start for another seven hours. I was in the second group.

The line was long, hot and competitive. We all knew that going home after school without these tickets would result in some kind of parental retribution. If we failed to get these tickets then our parents would have to arrive at the game after a long day's work and stand in line themselves alongside the crowd of team parents from the competing side, or "the other side," as we called them. Yes, we school kids who sacrificed our lunch time in order to buy tickets were giving our parents the ability to arrive at the basketball game later that night like VIP's, walking past the very long line and flashing their tickets to the ticket checkers with a smug and authoritative expression, as if they had been invited by the President of the United States to attend. In a small town, any upgrade or special treatment of any kind is taken extremely seriously.

Basketball is supposed to be a game of five on five. That wasn't the case when Central played a home game. We were allowed six. We weren't breaking any rules, and there was nothing the visiting team could do about it. You see, our basketball gym wasn't just any gym. In fact, it wasn't even called a "gym." It was known all over west Tennessee as "The Pit."

There weren't multiple entrances for convenience,

and there weren't multiple exists in case of an emergency. There was one way in and it was the same way out. Looking back, it was a guaranteed fire marshal nightmare. The Pit was constructed in such a way that the basketball court seemed more sunken down than normal and there was hardly any room to walk around it. The bottom row of the old creaky wooden bleachers was located practically on the out-of-bounds line of the court. The rest of the rows of seats were stacked almost on top of each other at an extremely steep incline, with no free walkways to get up and down, due to people sitting on them as if they were an extension of the bleachers. If you wanted to sit by your friend who was on the top row (literally in the rafters), you would have to step over the top of people who were smashed together shoulder to shoulder, sitting on every row between the floor and your friend. There was no air conditioning and there was no air flow. Temperatures from the compacted body heat would reach well into the 90's even if it was freezing cold outside, creating our very own locally brewed olfactory experience comprised of farm-boy body odor and cheap perfume. The only outside air that was able to make its way in came from a few horizontal, miniscule, sliver sized, hand crank windows that were located behind the top row of the home side seating. The "other side" had no relief whatsoever. These are the constructional facts about the gym where my high school's basketball games were played. And as intriguing and intimidating these facts may be to someone who has never heard of such a gym, there is more.

You see, our town saw these games as much more than "games." They were what we did. They were who we were. They were our identity. When I say our team was allowed six players, I'm talking about the fans. We bought up all the tickets so families from the visiting team who drove from afar to watch the game may not be able to get inside. We arrived early, not just to get a good seat, but to take up the visitors seating as well... with huge signs for our team that we planned on holding up so the unlucky people sitting behind us couldn't watch the game. While the other side was on the court warming up and our team was still in the locker room, our crowd was already cheering in anticipation of our hometown superstars taking the court. The other side would start looking suspicious, wondering why we would be so audibly aggressive when our team wasn't even visible yet. Like all the other girls, I remember each game I had picked out a new player to have a crush on. I would have visions of him falling down right in front of me in hopes that our eyes would meet, and that he would play the rest of the game in my honor to impress me. Yes, it's true. The boys on the basketball team at Obion County Central High School were absolute rock stars. I can still remember their names and which direction their hair was parted. They even had their own signature song. When it was time for our team to make their grand entrance onto to court, they didn't just step into our sight. "Jump" by Van Halen came across the loudspeaker, always turned up perfectly too loudly, and after a few seconds of the song playing, the team of twenty five majestic young men emerged from a sunken set of stairs, wearing all white jump suits, each of them dribbling their own basketball and going right into their choreographed warm-up, sending The Pit into full-blown ballistics. It was almost game time. Welcome to The Pit.

The crowd knew how the acoustics worked in The Pit, and we used them to our advantage. We didn't clap. We stomped. We didn't raise our hands when someone hit the three. We raised our fists. We didn't cheer. We yelled. And if this wasn't intimidating enough for the other side, we had people in the stands waving Confederate flags. Yes, the same flag that the Confederacy flew during the Civil War while fighting for their desire to be locally governed and to own slaves, was our actual high school flag. We even had a designated mascot who was a student with a Confederate flag so big, you could hear it flapping in the air as he ran circles around the court during timeouts. We yelled our Rebel Yell. Did it sound like Stonewall Jackson's 4th Virginia Volunteer Infantry Regiment at the First Battle of Bull Run when he commanded them to "Yell like furies!"? We don't know, but it was loud and it was vicious. To me it sounded like a cross between an angry pack of a thousand coyotes and clashing thunder that came in from hundreds of miles away just to be there. We were backwoods. We were ruthless, and we were mean. The referees had no grounds to shut us up-vocally supporting your team isn't against the rules and often, even the referees would seem afraid to make calls against us out of fear of being jeered by the crowd. In truth, there was probably good reason to be a bit scared. Our crowd was the gun-carrying kind, but we left them in our trucks during school events. Everyone who supported our team flew the Rebel flag and wore it on their shirt- not just the hundreds and hundreds of white people, but also the few black people, and the fewer brown people. We flew it and wore it together. We did everything together to support our team. We stomped so hard in unison that it felt like the very bricks that made up the walls were about to crumble down around us and then we stomped some more, with even greater intensity. That's right, if you were coming to a Central basketball game, you were committing to sweating together, suffering together, getting angry together, celebrating together and losing your voice and sense of hearing together. If you were part of the "The Pit", then you were part of the family, and if you weren't, then you were probably pissing your pants. The sheer force and volume of the cheers injected an inescapable fear into the most formidable opponents. It was at The Pit, flying the Confederate flag, where the all the voices in the community were in unison, regardless of race, color, and religion. Oh, the irony. But oh, the truth. These memories warm my heart with such sincere love and pride, yet make me shake my head at the unbelievability of it all. It's almost too much to handle. Nevertheless, it was what it was, and it is what it is.

Pitted Grilled Sugar Peaches with Boozy Bourbon Whipped Cream

Yield: 3-4 servings

- 6 peaches, halved, pits removed
- 1.5 cups granulated sugar
- 1.5 cups heavy whipping cream
- ½ cup confectioners sugar
- 2 Tbs. bourbon
- ¾ cup toasted pecans or walnuts (optional)

Spray a cast iron grill pan with cooking spray and place over medium heat (or cook on charcoal grill). Press and swirl the cut side of the peaches in the granulated sugar. Grill for 2-3 minutes in the grill pan until marks form and they achieve desired texture.

Beat the cream, powdered sugar and bourbon in a bowl with a mixer until soft peaks form.

Serve the peaches and whipped cream together in three or four individual cups or bowls, sprinkled with nuts if desired.

ASSEMBLY & EATING:

It's ladies' night at your home with 3 or 4 of your closest girlfriends that you've known since high school. Lay the servings out on the kitchen table. Tell the girls, who are on their third glass of wine, to get their tails off the couch and take the one they want or you'll eat theirs too. Tell them to hurry or the heat from the peaches will melt the cream. If they are moving too slowly, remind them there is bourbon in the recipe. They will laugh and walk faster. Open another bottle of wine. The night is young. Tell Heather that pouring straight bourbon on top of the peaches and cream does not count as "garnishing." Jump right into the debate. Who was cuter in high school? Chris or John? Chris. Always Chris. Ask Jennifer why she never returned your shirt from tenth grade. Demand that she better be wearing it the next time you see her. Laugh hard. Notice how even when their wrinkles show, all you see is who they were when you first met. Hug them for no damn reason, which is the perfect reason. You feel they are softer and rounder, but all you see is that high school cheerleader size four. Be thankful that they are there, and that you are together. Be thankful that you can go over the memories still. Be thankful for Grilled Sugar Peaches and Boozy Bourbon Whipped Cream.

CHAPTER SEVENTEEN

COLD FEET ON THE FLOOR

Cold feet on the floor, cold feet on the floor, phone hanging by a thread.

There's a voice on the line telling me he's gone.

You can't, you won't, but I need

The things you don't have to give.

And I come to terms with the emptiness

that only the song understands.

And as I start to turn it off,

I turn it up instead,

and stared, and breathed, and cried the tears

you never knew I had

because

you can't, you won't, but I need

the things you don't have to give.

When he called home, I listened

from across the room

when it came time for him to say, "goodbye."

Bravery and courage cowardly stowed away

on a no bound plane when I needed to be strong,

leaving me alone on the family floor

to sort through the things

you shouldn't think about when you're a kid.

And so I rock, rock, rock, myself

because

you can't, you won't, but I need

the things you don't have to give,

the things you don't know how to give,

the things you weren't given too.

Cold feet on the floor, cold feet on the floor, phone hanging by a thread.

GOD, SEE GODSEY

"You're making a mistake," they said- my parents, my teachers, and even my coaches. "You're not supposed to be in the band." The Obion County Central High School marching band was over two hundred students strong, and had just won the state marching band competition. Their drum major was a senior who was on his way out. Auditions for the position were announced. I spent days that turned into weeks imagining that I was standing in front of them, conducting their signature warm up song, "Take My Hand, Precious Lord," and feeling the brass line pin my ears back with their fortissimo as my hands pounded out the 3-4 time with all of my strength. The thought of doing that felt good. It felt inspiring. It felt... *right*.

The last drum major was a guy and he was considered "the best." "They'll want another guy again," everyone said of the new drum major. It was true- the last drum major was "the best." He won every award with the exception of just a couple that were so out of our band's league that no one even considered it a loss. In any band competition, the band directors actually counted on his high marks to make up for possible low ones that the band would get in other areas, bringing the overall score up enough for the band to get ranked among bands that, under any other circumstances, they would not be able to stand toe to toe with, so to speak. He was "the best." Everyone tried to convince me that there was no point in me trying out. They all tried to tell me to spend my time doing other things in school, like clubs and sports, so I thought about not auditioning. I closed my eyes and put my head down in different places: my bedroom, the classroom, my car. I tried to listen for something that I didn't know had a sound. I tried to hear the sound of *right*. With my eyes closed and a few deep breaths, I could picture myself *not* in the band. I could picture myself with other people, doing other things. I could hear their voices and feel the air. It felt the same way it did when I first lifted my head on the school bus and saw my selection of seating partners. It felt the same way it did when I saw the dirty garden hose Peggy was drinking out of at her house. It felt the same way it did when I learned about Kingdom. It felt empty with an overall feeling of dread. It felt... *wrong*. I had to obey my instincts.

I mustered up the guts to tell the adults in my life that I was going to go against their advice that they had taken time to give me with love. It was hard. I usually did what adults said, and I didn't like to disappoint people. One conversation after another, I was faced with the disapproval of my choice by the adults that I cared so much for and who cared for me. I started second guessing myself. How can I be doing the right thing when so many people disagree? I just needed the judges to take a chance on me, even though I was a girl, even though "the best" had been a guy. I knew if they picked me, I wouldn't let them down. I would practice until I was the best too. I would outwork every drum major on the east coast of the United States to prove they didn't make a mistake by picking me, and to prove to everyone I made the right choice by auditioning.

The day for auditions came. The guy who was known as "the best" was there, probably to intimidate any new people who were wanting to take his coveted place. Our band directors were there and they had invited their music professor friends from the local college, the University of Tennessee at Martin, to sit in as well. There were also band members sitting in the room with very judgmental eyes, just to watch and be… judgmental. All in all, there were about fifty people in the room, waiting for each hopeful to walk in and conduct a musical track of our choice to an imaginary orchestra. It was a big make-believe merry-go-round that would determine our future in the band and, potentially, our reputation in the school. Around twelve people were vying for the drum major position, a mix of guys and girls. Everyone had practiced for weeks to conduct their song, some of them even obtained private lessons... I wasn't the private lesson type. I had watched "the best" before and took mental notes and just applied them to my song. I remember hoping that the routine I made up translated into proper conducting. I really didn't know. I was slot number eleven, which meant I had to wait in the same room for a very long time with my competitors as they were called one by one. It was the same process over and over. A knock came on the door, a student would exit, we would hear their song of choice being played loudly which meant they were conducting. Some time would pass. Then, they would come back red as a beet from nerves. After forty minutes of this torturous process, it was now my turn. I walked out, stepped on the platform, stated my name and thanked the judges for considering me. A senior in the back cued up my song and nodded to confirm that the track was ready. I knew song choice was going to be key. I wanted to really stand out. I knew everyone else would make predictable selections from *Les Miserables*, *Fiddler on the Roof, Phantom of the Opera* or maybe a John Phillips Sousa song.

I put my hands in the air to begin the routine. "Can you turn it up a bit louder?" I asked before giving the cue to start. He did, and nodded.

The a cappella voices that begin the song are unmistakable. The harmonies are hypnotizing as they melt together like 5 different colors of glittery candle wax being poured into a glass container. They remain perfectly balanced and mixed until the solo begins after the piano and bass guitar enter. No, I had not chosen a classical orchestral piece to conduct. I had chosen Queen's "Bohemian Rhapsody" and I had choreographed a routine that would show off an elegant 4-4 pattern, along with my ability to direct time changes, and of course, to conduct and head bang simultaneously. That's right. I didn't know if I was going to get this new drum major position, but I had decided that I was going to conduct the heck out of Freddie Mercury, putting his voice and the band at the mercy of my raw, untrained conducting fingertips. Four minutes and seven seconds into the song, the majority of the room was head banging with me while I conducted the most jamming 4-4 pattern I could push out. When the song was over, I didn't know if I had won the coveted position, but I knew I had set myself up for a great year in band. The judges thanked me and I walked out of the room feeling like I was soaring through the sky. When it was all said and done the Band Directors, Mrs. Hernon and Mr. Godsey, had chosen me and two other girls to lead the band as a united front, and we did. Stacy, Keleia, and I worked everyday after school on our routine and on our salute. Our practices long outlasted those of the football team, as sometimes we would see them packing up to go home when we had decided we needed to stay another two hours. The way we mapped out and planned our strategy of how to march two hundred kids onto football fields all over Tennessee and get them off before half-time was over, was nothing short of James Bond skill level. It was like arranging a pound of black-eyed peas into perfect rows in a pot of simmering water- it seemed impossible, but we learned and we did it. We went on to shatter the scores of the previous "best" and even took home the awards that they guy before us didn't. Those who had tried to dissuade me from trying out for the band eventually became my biggest supporters and would cheer the loudest in the stands. I had taken a big chance to audition, and Mrs. Hernon and Mr. Godsey took a chance on me. The three of us worked our tails tirelessly to deliver. We practically lived in the band room. We were always carrying a change of clothes, snacks and a toothbrush. Sometimes we even had pillows so we could take a short nap just to wake up and practice a few more hours, so when it was announced that Mr. Godsey had become very ill, it was a devastation to us. Not just to us, but to everyone in the band, including all the additional teachers and all of our parents. Most of the students did not know how to deal with it. The band parents helped us stay strong and cope through our practices and performances. That's what we did. We were family. We all prayed that he would be healed and not have to leave us. We prayed that God would see Mr. Godsey, and not take him away from us. Even in his last breath he taught us something- that the day comes for all of us when that last breath is taken, and that nothing lasts forever.

Smoky Black-Eyed Peas

Yield: 8-10 servings

- 1.5 pounds fresh black-eyed peas, rinsed
- 1 smoked piece of meat (ham hock, turkey leg or chicken wings)
- 3 cups water
- 2 cups unsalted chicken broth
- 3 garlic cloves, minced
- 1 Tbs. soy sauce
- 2 tsp. ground black pepper
- ¼ tsp. crushed red pepper

ASSEMBLY & EATING:

In a Dutch oven or medium pot, bring all the ingredients to a boil. Turn the heat down to a simmer. Cook for an hour until the peas are tender, stirring every 15 minutes. Remove the meat from the pot and shred from the bone. Add the meat back into the peas and stir before serving.

Discard the bone… or don't. You can actually freeze it in a freezer-safe storage bag to throw in a pot of boiling water with root vegetables and a bay leaf at another time should you, or your kids, or your neighbor falls ill.

It makes an excellent restorative sipping broth. It's also great in other soup or stew recipes that call for water. Replacing the water with this savory and smoky broth will add a new dimension to your dish. It will have the church ladies at the Sunday afternoon potluck wondering what you did this time to make your chili so special. You *could* tell them, or you could keep it a secret. But if you ask me, you might want to let that secret ride for a bit... you know Ms. Massey didn't give you the right amount of eggs and butter in her Sour Cream Pound Cake recipe at the last revival- and you still haven't called her out on it. Just sayin'.

CHAPTER EIGHTEEN

THE RESCUE BELL

A hundred hands grabbing.

No ground beneath my feet.

The sound of voices never ending.

No comfort in the sheets.

And I would like to call for rescue

if only I had a phone,

but instead the bell came ringing,

coming to bring me home.

And the mighty giants

who lay sleeping with their snores,

had no idea that outside

I was being so adored,

because when they three did breathe

made a peculiar tone,

did cover up the sound of the bell

that came to bring me home.

And when the singing and dancing was done

and over in the streets,

I went inside, slipped off the slippers

once on my Nanay's feet,

and joined the chorus of snoring giants

creating my very own tone,

and dreamt of the sound of the bell

that came to bring me home.

SOUTHERN GIRL IN AN ASIAN WORLD

Loud. Busy. Crowded. I felt someone pulling my shirt while another person tried to take a picture with me. My mom grabbed my right elbow and my aunt grabbed my left. My grandmother, who I called "Nanay," led the way. They started shouting to the crowd in Tagalog and pushing through the mass of people in order to get to the baggage claim area. I could feel myself breathing hard, and the skin of my eyes pushed back more than normal as I opened them as widely as I could out of nervousness.

"You think you can do this for two weeks?" my mom shouted towards me, trying to speak in a volume that was louder than the crowd, before breaking out into what I considered inappropriate laughter.

I wanted to go home, and I wanted to scream it at the top of my lungs. I wanted to escape the arms of my mom and aunt and turn around and jump back on the plane, even though I didn't know where it was going. I wanted to escape. I wanted to run. I wanted to hide. This wasn't a haunted house or a strange sort of intervention. This was the Manila International Airport, and we had just stepped off the plane onto Philippine soil.

"Why are they all trying to touch me?" I asked my mom. She laughed.

"They think you're famous," she said.

"Why would they think that?" I asked in an almost panicked tone. She laughed again while simultaneously pulling my arm and pushing through the crowd.

"They just do," she said. And that was the explanation for every question I would ask for the next two weeks while I was in the Philippines with my mom, aunt, and grandmother. I had never been out of the United States before, and I didn't speak any language other than English. After the plane landed, I never knew exactly where on a map I was, and I never knew where I was going next. I was at the mercy of the decisions of my family with absolutely no input or understanding about what was happening, or what was happening next. I felt like a full grown toddler.

"Why do they want me to touch their hand to my forehead?" I'd ask.

"They just do."

"Why do they let the mice run all over the place like that?" I'd ask.

"They just do."

"Why do they want me to be a Godparent to their child when they don't even know me?"

"They just do."

"Why do they drink soda from a plastic bag?"

"They just do."

"Why do they call every brand of toothpaste Colgate?"

"They just do."

"Why do they want to marry me when we haven't even spoken?"

"They just do."

It was the trip of "They just do." It was hard. I was told the trip was a combination of a high school graduation gift and an eighteenth birthday present- a "girls trip"- a rite of passage of sorts, where we would enjoy nice hotels and the benefits of cheap shopping. It wasn't. It was night after night of sleeping on dirt floors with mice and feeling incredibly tricked and all alone, even though everyone who saw me wanted to be within touching distance of me, all the while trying to be respectful to my elders and trying not to cry. The culture shock was intense. I didn't eat for days and the very thought of food made me nauseous. The struggle to just get by, hour by hour, was very real, and although my mom was proud to show me off, she seemed to somewhat enjoy watching my torment, as if she thought I had all of this "coming to me" as penance for what she called my popular and privileged life back in Tennessee. There was nothing I could do about it. I had to endure.

I woke up one morning while everyone else was still sleeping. On this particular day, we were fortunate to be staying with a relative who had a bed for us, and I mean "us." My mom, grandmother, aunt and I all laid on the bed next to each other. We decided before falling asleep that laying horizontally would give us more room, so that's what we did. Having my body on a mattress was such a luxury that I barely noticed that our heads were resting on our arms in the absence of pillows, and our feet were all dangling off the side of the bed, suspended in the air. Our bodies were all pushed up against one another. No matter which way I turned, I was pressed up against the curvy pillowy flesh that only a mature woman's body can offer. Snoring. Lots of snoring. I listened as if it were a song, as if I could learn more about their personalities by the way they breathed while they were unconscious. A rooster crowed outside even though it was still dark. I could hear the early morning conversations of the neighbors leaving for their morning walk to the local outdoor market. I heard a dog bark. It sounded weak and hungry. Everything in the air was so foreign to me, yet the snores of the two generations of women sleeping beside me said, "We're home." Then came an unexpected familiar sound in the distance. My eyes looked up. My ears scanned the atmosphere outside in hopes of hearing it again. There it was! Louder! It brought an unexplainable happiness that I had not felt since I arrived in the Philippines. I carefully sat up. The sleeping women beside me were unaffected. I slipped on my grandmother's rhinestone flip flops, and made my way to the front door, where I held my hand on the knob for quite some time, contemplating courage. This was the first time in the country that I took the initiative to go somewhere without my mother's permission. I was scared and not properly dressed. The sun was rising. On the other side of the door was a world where I didn't speak the language and I knew no one, but the sound was calling me, even louder now. It was right on the other side, waiting for me. I took a shaky breath, and turned the knob. I squinted my eyes and pulled the door open, ever so slowly. It opened to reveal the waking world that I was just listening to, frozen in place looking back at me. The people, the dog, the rooster- all frozen looking at me, standing in the door with squinty swollen morning eyes and bushy hair in my perfectly matched tank top and shorts pajamas. Silence. I looked around, not remembering what I was doing, and then, RING RING! The sound. I lifted my chin to attention and saw a boy on a bike, about my age, maybe a bit younger. He had the same bike bell as my friend Teresa! I slowly shuffled over to him, to see if indeed the bell was the same. When I got close, he smiled and rang it again. RING RING! *Dancing baby stars flying out of a glitter baton, about to grant a wish!* I smiled and exhaled so passionately that I almost cried. He rang it again. I touched it gently with my fingers. I noticed he was pulling a cart behind his bike. He got off of the seat and flipped open a metal lid and put a scoop of purple ice cream into a cone, and extended it towards me. I had never seen purple ice cream before, and I certainly had never eaten ice cream as the sun was rising, but I believed it was a sign. I held my index finger up as if to say, "Hold on" and I ran inside to grab money from my purse located near the door. I handed him a dollar and I waited for him to hand me the ice cream, but when he saw what I handed him, he revealed an enormous smile with missing teeth and held it in the air to waive it like a celebratory flag. People started approaching the cart to see. In my morning weariness, I had mistakenly handed him a United States ten dollar bill for one scoop of ice cream. He piled three more scoops onto the cone and handed it to me. Everyone watched and waited. I took my first bite with hesitation, slurping the top to try and understand what flavor it could possibly be. It was cold and refreshing. My taste buds began to wake with interest. The next bite revealed a heartiness to it, unlike any American ice cream I had ever had. Then it was smooth and comforting, like a Thanksgiving pie. It was everything that a first meal after an unintentional three day fast should be. It was delicious and easy to eat. It was good to my soul. I raised my eyebrows to look at him in approval with my mouth still in the vibrant purple pile of cream that I was struggling to keep out of my nose. I took the next bite with confidence and energy, making it clear that I was going to tackle all four scoops right there in the street, to which the crowd emitted an audible cheer. And so I did. While my grandmother, mother, and aunt were asleep and snoring in the bed, I was in the streets of the Philippines wearing my pajamas, watching the sun come up with the locals, and eating four scoops of purple yam ice cream for breakfast while the crowd cheered me on. When I was finished, I wiped my ice cream dripped forearms off on my pajamas, took the hands of the elders around me and ceremoniously touched them to my forehead "just because." I thanked the boy on the bike, went back inside, removed my grandmother's slippers, and slipped back into bed with my sleeping family, and took my rightful place as the third generation in the snoring chorus because I finally felt like I was home.

Ube Ice Cream (Purple Yam Ice Cream)

Yield: 1 quart ice cream

- 1-2 purple yams
- 1 (13.5oz) can full fat coconut milk
- 1 cup heavy whipping cream
- 1/4 cup honey
- 1 tsp. sugar
- pinch sea salt

Peel and cut 1-2 purple yams. Boil them until soft, and allow to cool. Blend the yams in a food processor. Leave 1 cup of yams in the processor, and set aside the overage (if any) for another purpose. Add coconut milk, whipping cream, honey, sugar and sea salt to the yams in the food processor and blend until combined. Follow the directions on your ice cream maker and churn for 15-20 minutes or until it is the desired consistency. Transfer to a 1 quart freezer safe container to store up to two months.

ASSEMBLY & EATING:

Through personal experience I have learned that I cannot make this in advance. I once had a really great idea to use this at a small ladies' tea I was hosting along with some white chocolate macadamia cookies to make ice cream sandwiches. The contrast of the purple ice cream against the white cookies was going to be epic. Apparently in the middle of the night, I decided to take one little bite- you know, to make sure it was good, and I ended up eating more than I intended. When it came time to make the sandwiches, my friend Laura opened the container to see that it was only over halfway full. "Well, Dalena. Why don't you eat up all the purple ice cream, why don't you?" I had forgotten about my midnight escapade to the freezer and there was clear evidence proving that it had gotten out of hand. I felt reckless and irresponsible, like when you find out you're going to go on a date with a guy you really, *really* like and you swear to yourself that all you're going to do at the end of the night is kiss, and then the next thing you know you're wondering if you buttoned your shirt straight before you walk back into the house. Well, I had clearly failed to button my ube ice cream shirt back correctly. And Laura called me out on it. It was clear the girls wanted an explanation. If this ever happens, compose yourself as I did. Give everyone a spoon and just pass the carton around. Look at them, shrug your shoulders and say, "I don't kiss and tell."

CHAPTER NINETEEN

BREAK HAND BLUES

Break hand blues, factory shoes, a girl in our midst

Fifty thousand feet with wings, no Aquatred is missed

Black tar air, no resting chair, the second break bell tone

Black rubber tire soldiers, marching to go home

Fathers, mothers, sisters and brothers, back to do it again

Same today as yesterday, side by side with your friend

All of us in it together, with our own personal dreams

To be a coach, cook, cop or spy, and one who wants to be queen.

"TIRED" HANDS

I kept my eyes closed and my head down, standing perfectly still as the clean hot water ran down the back of my weary neck and shoulders. Was there a muscle in my body that didn't hurt? I mustered up the energy to barely open my eyes and look down towards my feet where the water was running down the shower drain. Black. All I saw was black liquid swirling over and over, making its way over the tops of my feet, channeling through the shallow grout crevices and disappearing past the place where it doesn't matter.

For the past two years of my life, I had been surviving the only way I knew how, which was the only way I could- the hard way. I had been completely on my own since I turned eighteen and moved out of my parents' house. I was paying for everything I had and everything I wanted: all of my own college tuition, books, car insurance, school supplies, gas for my car, health insurance, groceries, clothes, rent and all the bills that come along with being a tenant. I was a full-time student at the University of Tennessee at Martin, working three part-time jobs, which allowed me to be able to afford a run down apartment that I shared with a gay duck hunter who liked to write poetry and loved the color blue. Sometimes at the end of a long day, I'd come home to find him happily sitting on the couch, reading a book by candlelight with a bag of candy that he would hold up in my direction as I walked in the door, barely able to take another step.

"You know your candy bag greeting is the best part of my day," I'd say, dropping my purse heavily on the floor, throwing my weary body on the couch next to him, taking a Twizzler from the bag and placing it in my mouth, not knowing if I had the energy to chew.

"You know you can't keep working this hard, Dalena. You're too young and pretty. You're twenty years old, taking twenty three hours a semester, and working three jobs. It's too much! Why do you do so much?" he asked.

"It's the only way. I don't have anyone paying my bills. If I take this many hours, I'll graduate early, saving me a semester of tuition and books. I work this many jobs to pay my bills. It's just me, man. Just me," I replied.

"Well, something's gotta give," he said. "I mean, shit. We need to move to a better place, but I know you can't afford it. Did you have to sleep with pots and pans in the bed last night again because of the rain storm?" he asked.

"Yep, got a full three hours of sleep," I responded. "I figured out that if I put sponges in the pots, then the rain doesn't make as much noise." There was silence. "Our landlord is a jerk."

"Yeah," he agreed. "Sorry you drew the bad bedroom."

"It's okay," I responded.

"Another Twizzler, honey?" he asked, extending the bag my direction.

"Sure," I said with a smile.

This conversation is the reason why I was so happy to be accepted into the summer program at the Goodyear tire factory for college students. Yes, it was the same factory where my father was working when I was born, and he was still working there at this time. It meant I could quit my three minimum wage part-time jobs, and work full-time making over ten dollars an hour. I didn't take summer classes, so not only would I not have to worry about school, I could take as much overtime as I could get, which would put me in the eighteen dollar an hour range. It was exciting. My whole future was about to change. I had visions of being able to go to the grocery store and buying a ribeye steak, A1 sauce, and French bread without worrying about the price. I could fill my car up with gas instead of constantly surviving on a quarter of a tank. Maybe I could even try a better brand of face wash and powder makeup. It felt like a whole new world was upon me.

I spent as many hours at the factory as I could, doing the best I could because I wanted to be the first college student considered for overtime when it became available. The first job they gave me was called "sorting." I pushed tires onto their corresponding conveyor belt based on their type. Then I got "promoted," which meant I stood in front of an even bigger conveyor belt beside four men. My job was to pick up as many tires as I could and stack them in a zigzag pattern on a rolling pallet, until it was so high that I couldn't throw any more on top. Then I would get a fresh empty pallet and do it all over again. It was hard physical labor that not many of the other college kids who were accepted could handle. The tires varied in size. A few types I could pick up easily because they were as light as a feather, and some were so big and heavy that I could sit inside of them. It didn't matter. I had to pick them up and stack them, and I did.

And that's where the black in the shower came from. My father was coughing it up twenty-one years ago, and I was coughing it up now. It was good money. No, it was great money. My father supported our entire family off of this kind of money. I only had to support me. The managers there told me that if quit college, I could make a career working in the factory. They told me I could make over fifty thousand dollars a year stacking tires- that I could have holidays off or get paid *triple* time. They told me I would get paid vacation time off, and a few days paid sick leave. Factory life was never my dream, but every time I got paid and saw my check, I thought about it. I could buy a new car. I could pay bills without wondering if the check would clear. Maybe if I lived extremely frugally, I could even retire young, but every night after work I had a reminder of why that couldn't be, and it was black. It was the black rolling down my body in the shower and down the drain. It was the black that made me cough so hard that I wondered if I needed medicine. It was the black balls of tar that I would find in my hair the morning after my shower, when I thought I was clean. It was the black on my hands that never really came off. Black was imbedded into my fingerprints, telling me "no." They had become "tired," so to speak. I knew I had to make as much money as I could in the summer and then go back to school.

One day I was at Walmart buying a new bandana to keep my hair back off of my face at work when I heard a happy group of girls in the aisle next to me.

"You know the Miss University of Tennessee at Martin pageant will be coming up after we go back in the fall. Queen wins a scholarship for tuition and books," one girl said.

"Yeah, if only I was motivated to go to the gym three hours a day to get in shape," said the other.

They walked past me to leave the store. I thought about their conversation for a good hard minute. Then I put back the box of Little Debbie Swiss rolls and grabbed a bag of apples instead.

ar-Dusted Chili Ribeye

- 3 Tbs. chili powder
- 3 large garlic cloves, chopped and mashed to a paste with 1 tsp. salt
- 3½ Tbs. Soy Sauce
- 1.5 tsp. ground cumin
- 1 tsp. sugar
- Four (12 -16 ounce) rib eye steaks (12 oz. for boneless or 16 oz. bone-in)

Mix the first five ingredients together in a bowl. Rub both sides of each steak with the paste. Place in a large sealable plastic bag. Place in the refrigerator to marinate for 4 hours. Remove steaks from refrigerator 45 minutes before grilling, preferably over charcoal. The key to getting the "char" is a hot grill. Grill until preferred doneness. Remove from grill and let rest for 4 minutes before eating.

ASSEMBLY & EATING:

Sometimes "black char" will develop and stick to the tongs or spatula during the cooking process. Scrape it off with a butter knife, dust a tiny bit of it onto your hot sizzling steak, then spread it in using no greater force than a feather blowing gently in the breeze. It will melt with the juices and disappear into invisible, barely noticeable, bitter black deliciousness. With each bite, try to find it in the flavor. You will find other flavors while you search, causing your eating journey to be that much more enjoyable, like when you go hiking to reach the top of Lookout Hill, but are surprisingly more entertained by the flowers and birds along the way. You deserve this steak. You've been working hard. Your muscles work harder than the average person's and it's catching up with you. Crack open a cold beer, pour a glass of your favorite wine, or put extra ice in your sweet tea while you're at it. It's been a long day and you're about to eat a beautiful, hot, sizzling steak from the grill.

CHAPTER TWENTY

LOST AT ALL COST

No clue what to do.

Don't even know how to buy shoes.

How high? To the sky?

No lesson lent on lining eyes.

Bought the dress, but what a mess.

Was never taught a beauty process.

Out of my league, much indeed.

No training knowledge on how to proceed.

Lost at all cost.

Uncharted territory, my boss.

Hunting courage, but feeling frail.

The hope of help, my only avail.

BEAUTY QUEEN MAKING MACHINE

"Of course the beauty school drop out will do your hair!" she said with excitement. Mindy was my friend who I had known since before high school. She dropped out of college at UTM to go to cosmetology school. It proved quickly to be the right decision. All the popular sorority girls and guys would make appointments with her in between their classes and before special events. Mindy did hair, nails, makeup... anything one may need in the realm of beauty, Mindy was the girl to get and the girl everyone wanted. I dropped by her apartment without warning to inquire about possible pageant hair services to find that her little home based beauty shop venture had grown into a full blown enterprise with three appointments stacked back to back, a scheduled cigarette break, and then a haircut and manicure appointment afterwards. Her calendar was books for weeks in advance. We sat on the back porch together. She tucked a wad of cash in her bra before lighting up a Virginia Slim. I chuckled.

"Girl, you are running a full blown business up in here," I said.

"I know that's right," she said blowing her menthol cigarette smoke opposite of my direction. "Hold on, this is my jam!"

Her TV was turned to BET. She raised the roof with her cigarette hand while she turned up the volume with the remote in the other, then she came back outside. I leaned back in the broken lawn chair that I was sitting in, folded my arms, and grinned with my eyebrows raised as she began rapping every word to The Notorious B.I.G.'s "Mo Money Mo Problems" while continuing to smoke her cigarette and dance. Oh, this Mindy. I just loved her.

"You got a dress?" she asked, while doing the percolator and waving to a neighbor who was taking out his trash.

"Yeah, I don't know what else I need though. I'm not sure how these things work. This is a serious pageant."

"You know who you need, don't ya?" she asked. "Natalie."

When it came to pageants in West Tennessee, she could only be talking about one Natalie. No last name was needed. She was a beautiful blonde niece of a State Representative who walked on stage like her daddy discovered the entire state of Tennessee. If she showed up backstage to compete in a pageant, everyone else might as well have gone home. The girl just shined. We had hung out a few times with mutual friends, and I just loved her. She wasn't pretentious at all. She had great taste in music and had the funniest sense of humor. She was always willing to share anything she had, but I felt uncomfortable asking her for help. I didn't know if we were on good enough terms for me to ask her for pageant secrets. I called her, and before I could even get the question out of my mouth, Natalie told me I didn't need another thing. She had everything I needed, down to the Swarovski crystal chandelier earrings.

I had spent three months that summer at Goodyear making as much money as I could while throwing tires to get in shape, and surviving on a strict diet of turkey slices, apples and water. By the time the pageant rolled around, I was a svelte size four with a six pack, cut arms, and black hair down to my waist. Those "Big Ballerina Pork Chop Days" were gone with the wind. I wasn't playin'. I wanted to win this scholarship. If I did, I wouldn't have to work so much and I could study more and try to bring up my GPA.

Natalie came to meet me at Mindy's a few days before the pageant for planning and coaching. She arrived wearing mirrored aviator sunglasses and red lipstick, carrying garment bags, shoe boxes and makeup cases like she had just robbed a mall.

"Did you bring everything you own?" asked Mindy, with her hand on her hip, holding a curling iron. Natalie looked up bewildered.

"No, I just brought a couple of things."

We spent two hours in Mindy's living room playing with my hair, walking and turning in shoes, trying on my dress with pantyhose, then without pantyhose. Occasionally Natalie and Mindy would argue about which earrings worked better, or whether I should go with a closed or open toe shoe, but everything finally got decided. I didn't know how I could possibly be prepared any better than this.

It was pageant day and over twenty girls arrived to compete.

"Hey, girl! I didn't know you were going to be here!" one contestant said to another. "Good to see you! Let me get my momma to take a picture of us." The girls hugged and posed. This is what I saw for thirty minutes backstage before the pageant began. It was clear. Most of these girls knew each other. They were professional pageant girls and I was the sitting duck. How stupid could I be to think I could do this? To think that I had spent three months foolishly looking at the thousands and thousands of tires that came my direction as an opportunity for me to burn a calorie and define a muscle to win a scholarship. It made me want to cry off my makeup that Mindy so graciously applied for me with care and positivity. I thought about the Philippines- if I could hold in my tears in one hundred degree plus weather in a foreign country and still smile, I could do it now too. Besides, my beautiful crepe and satin halter top dress with a sweetheart neckline and slit on the leg was white as snow, specifically chosen to contrast against my naturally tan skin color. It would be easy to ruin with mascara and tears. Not to mention, it was a rental.

"Who are you?" I heard a voice coming from behind me in a slithering tone. I turned around to see a beautiful blond haired girl in a white dress with the most perfect bangs and winged black eyeliner I had ever seen.

"Dalena," I said.

"Oh, we were just talking," she said pointing to a cluster of other girls who clearly deemed her the spokesperson for the group. "We don't know you."

"Uh, no. This is my first time," I said.

"In a pageant?" she asked sharply with wide eyes.

"Uh no. I won second and third maid years ago," I

said.

"Oh really? Where?" she asked, intrigued.

"I was a little girl at the Obion County Fair and Hillcrest Elementary," I said almost ashamed. The girl bit her bottom lip to stop herself from laughing in my face although the girls in the corner couldn't help themselves. One of them almost spewed water from her nose onto her heavily beaded blue gown. I had an instant vision of punching this girl in the face, but I was saved when I was five and baptized at the First Baptist Church in Troy, so I couldn't.

"All of us know each other from the Strawberry Festival, Iris Festival, Soybean Festival, and the Banana Festival pageants."

"That's a lot of festivals," I said blandly.

"Well, good luck Darlene!" she said before rejoining her friends in the corner.

It was pageant time and we took our places. The music started. The emcee began speaking in a vibrant, energetic tone. We all took a breath and walked out to introduce ourselves in the microphone. Then came our individual walks. I hit all of my marks and turned just the way Natalie taught me to. Then we were brought out on stage in groups and instructed to do quarter turns. I could feel my cheeks shaking from holding the smile for so long. I wondered if the judges could see it. Then at the final quarter turn to face the judges again, the emcee announced that they had a surprise portion of the competition: Q & A.

Whatever that thing is inside of me, and inside of you, that knows something when we know it without explanation, got activated. The air surrounding the "festival girls" deflated like a lead balloon, and the other underdog contestants instantly stood a little taller. I knew what it meant. The "festival girls" couldn't speak into a microphone to save their lives. My eyes met the gaze of a beautiful black girl who also didn't have much pageant experience. We looked at each other with respect. We agreed with our eyes: there was hope for us! The blonde girl was called to the microphone.

"If you could a erect a statue on the UTM campus in anyone's honor, who would it be and why?" she was asked. She froze up as she looked into the crowd with her perfect winged eyeliner.

"My grandma, because she's the nicest person I know," she said.

"Did you grandmother attend college here?" asked the emcee.

"No," she said confidently, holding her pageant stance and smile, waiting to be excused from the stage.

And this is how the interview portion continued with all the "pros." It was the underdogs who were most composed with eloquent answers. My heart swelled for them as they slayed their questions. Then came my turn. I stepped up to the mic.

"If you could change anything about UTM what would it be?" I knew my answer immediately.

"I would change how scholarships are distributed among the students. If you are a decent student and your major is in a department with a lot of funding, there is a good chance that you can get a scholarship to pursue that major, but that doesn't mean that person is necessarily a better student than anyone else. It just means he or she chose a well-funded major. There are many great students that go to school here that are majoring in an area with very little funding for scholarships. We need students to continue choosing those majors so the departments can stay open. The best way to do that is to restructure the scholarship programs so the university can offer financial help to those dedicated students, like myself who have decided to pursue a major that doesn't get as much funding, like Communications and Theater. Thank you."

The crowd, which was mostly filled with students, gave me a strong applause, and when it was all said and done, the beautiful black girl won first maid and I was named Miss University of Tennessee at Martin. It was the first crown that had ever been placed on my head. I looked up and silently thanked God for every one of those tires that rolled my way down the conveyor belt that summer. I changed out of my dress and put on my sweat suit, packed up my things backstage, and jumped in the car with Mindy and Natalie. We celebrated by going to Taco Bell and obnoxiously rapping the incorrect words to whatever Mindy deemed was the appropriate song of the moment while we driving around town.

The next week I got a surprising call from my manager at Goodyear. He called to tell me that the second and third shift crews at the factory hung up the front page of the newspaper that featured a bright shining picture of me winning the title in the break room. He held up the phone for me to hear a few of my past coworkers congratulating me. I put my head down and closed my eyes to listen. I looked down at my hands which were now soft, clean, and manicured. I remembered the days when it seemed like they would always be dirty, black, and "tired", not knowing that they were actually the hands of a queen.

Grilled Granny Smith Apple & Turkey Sandwiches on Rye

Yield: 4 sandwiches

- 1 Tbs. Dijon mustard
- 1 Tbs. honey
- Dash fresh cracked pepper
- 8 (1-ounce) slices rye bread
- 4 (1-ounce) slices Swiss cheese
- 1 Granny Smith apple, sliced thinly to your preference
- ½ stick soft butter
- 8 ounces sliced deli turkey breast

Combine mustard, honey and black pepper in a bowl. Spread inside surface of two pieces of bread with the spread. Assemble the sandwich: layer cheese, apple and turkey, on top of the spread side. Place the other piece of bread spread side down on top of the sandwich. Coat both sides of the sandwich with soft butter. Repeat the process to make the rest of the sandwiches. Heat a large nonstick skillet to medium-high. Drop another little pat of butter into the skillet and let the butter melt. Cook sandwiches until bread is toasted to your liking and cheese melts, about 2 minutes.

ASSEMBLY & EATING:

Please don't be a fool and think that because there are paper thin apples sitting on top of turkey that this can in any way be considered "health food." Clearly, this is not the sandwich to eat if you are on a diet. The butter alone will cause the treadmills at your gym to malfunction and lock up when you walk past them in the morning to work this off. The cheese and bread will be no cakewalk to work off either. If you decide to make this, just commit to the calorie, carb and dairy intake, hunker down on your sofa like a bear in the winter, and don't make any plans to wear your swimsuit the next day. Oh, and since you're going to follow these instructions, then you might as well eat two. After all, there are apples in it.

CHAPTER TWENTY-ONE

NOT TONIGHT

Colors blinding your sight

Air puffed pupils extending the light

3-D glasses in the night

20-20, but you're not right.

Your anger it did ignite

When the color choice not white

Left you slumped and not upright.

I'd say sorry, but not tonight.

A BROWN MAGGIE

"But Maggie is supposed to be white!" a girl yelled. I stood around the corner from the posted cast list. I couldn't believe it either. I auditioned for Tennessee Williams's *Cat on a Hot Tin Roof* at my college and I had been cast as the lead female, played in the movies by Elizabeth Taylor and Jessica Lange. After I saw my name posted for the role of "Margaret", I ran around the corner to hide, but I wasn't sure why. Others were coming by to check the cast list too, unaware that I was just barely out of their sights, and could hear every word. I didn't want to be there necessarily. It's just that... I was frozen.

"Maggie isn't supposed to be white," said a male who was with her.

"Yes, she is! I read the script. It says it, plain as day! Maggie is supposed to be white! The entire family is white. All the lead parts are white! What we going to do? Have a *brown* Maggie?" asked the girl who had clearly auditioned.

"It's fine. Don't be so upset. Dalena will be good as Maggie," he said.

"I didn't say she wouldn't be good. I said Maggie is supposed to be white. The play takes place in the

Mississippi Delta on a plantation for crying out loud! If Tennessee Williams wanted a brown-skinned girl to play the part of Maggie, he would have said it in the script! Dalena looks like she just got off of the boat from Mexico. She should have been cast as one of slaves!" the girl exclaimed.

"You realize you don't have to take a boat from Mexico to get here, right?" the guy asked.

"Whose side are you on anyway?" she snapped back.

"There aren't sides, crazy. There's just a cast list, and you're not on it," he snapped back. "Oh look! I got cast as a slave! And I'm white."

"Uuugh! What a stupid cast!" she whined.

It sounded like she was going to cry. During auditions, I felt that my fellow hopefuls weren't taking me seriously for the lead. I didn't really put it together until I overheard that conversation. No one saw it coming. No one. Even at the first read-through, the director, Steve Riedel, admitted he didn't see it coming either, but in the end he thought I was the best choice. I had been in two other plays under his direction and with each play I was given a bigger role. This was the first time I had ever been cast as the lead, and there were some very mixed opinions about it.

I spent every spare minute I had in between classes

and my two jobs studying my lines. To say I studied my "lines" is actually an understatement. More accurately, I studied my paragraphs and pages. The script of *Cat on a Hot Tin Roof* looks a like a thick pamphlet full of Margaret or "Maggie" talking nonstop, page after page after page, and many of the key plot advancements and stage directions for other actors are contingent upon those lines being delivered at the appropriate time. I didn't like studying at my crappy apartment, so I found myself in the Fine Arts building rehearsing in the lab theater by myself, or hiding in the costume room with the Costume Director, Melanie Taylor, while she sewed our costumes by hand. She was playing the part of "Big Momma" and was always ready to give me acting notes and help me with script analysis whenever I asked.

Opening night came. One of the professors, Doug Cook, had transformed our theater stage into the most beautiful sprawling southern mansion boudoir, and I was about to spend the next forty-five minutes walking on it in a see-through slip under stage lights, talking nonstop in front of a packed house- white slaves and all. I went into a restroom stall to use it one last time before the show began and to double check my undergarments. As I secured my stocking into my garter belt, two girls entered the restroom.

"Well, we'll see," a girl said. "I think she's going to look ridiculous. She's just too dark for the part."

"I know. She's been working hard too. I feel sorry for her. It's like she doesn't realize no one wants her to be Maggie. She's just a goodie two shoes kiss ass, anyway. She should've dropped out and let a real actress have the part," the other said.

They were talking about me. My whole life I had been keeping my mouth shut about what people thought about me, and what they said to me. My whole life I rose above the naysayers. I had spent years doing what people said I wouldn't do, and *couldn't* do, working my tail off and making it look as easy as a summer's breeze. I never tried to rub people's noses in it, or make them feel bad for doubting me, or for underestimating me. Never. But these bitches caught me on the wrong damn day. I had a show to do, and it was time for places. I was not about to get in a bad headspace in this bathroom stall and have it ruin my performance. I felt heat rising up within me.

"Yeah! Who does she think she is anyway?" one of them asked.

I fiercely pushed the stall door open with both of my arms, stepped out and put my hands on my hips. I cocked my head to the side, and glared at them like I was going to cut 'em. They jumped up from leaning over into the mirror, gasped in fear to face me, stood shoulder to shoulder with their mouths wide open, as if they were going to beg for their lives. I took four slow steps towards them until we were face to face. I leaned over so close that my lips were almost touching their cheeks and I could see the corners of their eyebrows trembling.

"I'm a *brown* Maggie," I said, like I had a knife tucked into my garter belt. I leaned back, raised my eyebrows and looked at them as if to ask, "You gotta a problem with that?"

They didn't move a muscle.

"Didn't think so," I said as I slowly turned to wash my hands in the sink. "Now hand me a napkin."

And they did. Then I walked out while they stood in the same exact place I found them in, leaving them with a gracious, "Enjoy the show."

That night and every night was a success. Every performance was sold out, and some of us were invited north to compete in the Kennedy Center American College Theater Festival, where I placed in the top ten girls out of over three hundreds actors. I celebrated by enjoying my first ever glass of sangria in the Virginia rain.

When the play was over, I stopped by Steve's office during his office hours, where I knew I would find him and his wife Catherine, who was also teaching at the University. I thanked them for taking a chance on me, to which I expected to hear "the real story" of everything they endured for choosing me to play the role of Margaret, complete with details of the behind-the-scenes hardship that people gave them for their choice. I heard nothing of the sort. They responded with a loving smile and a very humble, "No problem, kid," to which I smiled back, nodded and left.

Cloved Virgin Sangria

Yields: about 1 gallon

- 1 (two liter) bottle ginger ale, chilled
- 1 bottle white grape juice (64 oz.)
- 3 ripe nectarines, sliced thinly
- 2 apples, sliced thinly
- 1 orange, sliced thinly
- 1/2 tsp. ground cloves

Thoroughly wash, dry, and slice all fruit and slice thinly, leaving the skin on. Place in a 1 gallon container. Pour juice over fruit. Refrigerate, covered, for at least 3 hours. When ready to serve, slowly pour in chilled ginger ale and stir.

Muscadine Sangria (Alcoholic)

- 1 (750ml) bottle muscadine wine (I use either Duplin Wine Cellars Sweet North Carolina Muscadine White Wine or Childress Vineyards American Muscadine Sweet White)
- 2 cups peach white grape juice
- 3 cups club soda

- 3/4 cup Shellback Silver Rum
- 3 peaches or nectarines, peeled & sliced
- 3 cups muscadine grapes, sliced in half
  (Pinot Grigio and white grapes can be substituted for the muscadine wine and muscadine grapes.)

ASSEMBLY & DRINKING:

Let me tell you this right now: this drink goes down easy, and because it's pretty, people underestimate it. Do not make this at a fancy dinner party among coworkers right before a possible promotion, because this alcoholic drink right here will have people LIT UP like a Fourth of July night sky over the General Jackson Showboat on the Cumberland River. It sneaks up and delivers a knockout punch to even the most experienced drinker. DO NOT, I repeat, DO NOT EVER, let anyone tell you that they "don't feel anything" and allow them to drive home because they "don't live too far away." You sit their tail down on your sofa, and let them play with their phone, channel surf... it doesn't matter... anything! Let them cross-stitch or knit a scarf for all I care, but YOU KEEP YOUR EYE ON THEM. I have seen the woes of a muscadine sangria night. It involved sun poisoning, a Michael Jackson song, and a group of my dorm room friends who, after this incident, became known as "The Pound Sisters." Muscadine sangria nights produce these types of stories that cause you to take oaths that will last over decades and decades and decades and keep you bonded to people. Be very selective about your drinking audience with this one. Very. The BIGGEST VERY that I can say. VEEEERRRRYYYY!

CHAPTER TWENTY-TWO

GOTTA GO

Cold Coffee, dirty dishes, vent broken by the door,

Hungry baby crying while I say, "We ain't got no more."

Boss man says I ain't trying, so I make another call.

Just to hear 'em say, "Not today, maybe in the fall."

There's gotta be, gotta be, something better than this.

Not asking for orphan Annie's dream, just something less killing than this.

I gotta go, go, go find the answers, to the things I never knew.

Who am I? Who am I?

And why?

Why am I? Why am I?

And Who?

Will I always be alone, or will I find love again?

Are the lines showing around my eyes? Will I be able to stay thin?

Will the bill stack ever shrink, or grow to bust through the roof?

What kind of mother will I make, can I teach my son to tell the truth?

What if I can't stop spinning in circles, what if my mind

resets to my youth?

How do I live calmly in this chaos, and become riot proof?

I gotta go, go, go find the answers, to the things I never knew.

Who am I? Who am I?

And why?

Why am I? Why am I?

And Who?

I'm thirsting for something with peaches, cheap bubbling zinfandel.

I'm at my wits' end with this dead water in my well.

I'm going to jump off this cliff onto I-40, and drive to the end,

Keep all my cards facing down, push all my chips in.

Baby bag full of diapers, suitcase full of dreams,

Bible in my glove box, old love letter up my sleeve.

I gotta go, go, go find the answers, to the things I never knew.

Who am I? Who am I?

And why?

Why am I? Why am I?

And Who?

GLADYS SAYS GO

After college, going where I had to for work and cheap rent was the way I survived and made ends meet. It had been a few years after graduating, and I found myself living as a single mother, renting a very old tiny brick house with a broken blue door in Union City. Moving into that house marked my eleventh move since being on my own when I turned eighteen, several years prior. There was an iron vent built into the floor that served as the source of heat when the months grew cold. Aslan, my baby boy, was just starting to walk and he would often step on the grate that was inconveniently placed right in front of his bedroom. He hated wearing any kind of socks or shoes, inevitably throwing them across the room when I wasn't looking, so as a result I would often just let it be cold in the house. I would rather snuggle under blankets than see grill marks on his precious little feet. I was out of a job and the bills kept coming. I had a four year college degree but there was nowhere in town to use it and make any higher of a salary than I did without it. Twice a month I made a dreadful trip to the consignment store to sell some of my best clothes and some of Aslan's favorite toys so I could have grocery money.

Hard life was becoming normal and I hated every minute of it. It was causing me a lot of stress. I would catch myself staring at the wall not realizing that my son had been pulling on my shirt, trying to get my attention. I felt like the town was trying to kill me by trapping me into being something that I didn't want to be. I was lost. I didn't know what to do. There was only one person who could soothe my woes and help me think straight.

"Is that your new car?" my grandmother asked as I stepped into her living room without knocking on her front door for an impromptu visit.

"Yes, it is. It's a Chevy Trailblazer," I said with a little regret. "I bought it before business went bad and now I'm stuck with the payment for the next four years. I can barely afford it. It's hard, Grandma."

"Nothing wrong with hard," she said. "Nothin' lasts forever. Besides, you deserve something new after all that time you were washin' and waxin' that totaled one." I was surprised she remembered my little Nissan Sentra that the insurance company wouldn't fix because the cosmetic repairs from a hit and run cost more than the car was worth. It ran fine, so I kept it clean and drove it for years anyway.

"How's Danny doing?" She asked.

"He's good, Grandma. His tomatoes and jalapeños look good this year."

"Well..." she'd say with a tilt of the head and a smile, stretching out the short "e" sound into two syllables that sounded more like a long "a." Her tone made it sound like she was saying, "That's great. I'm so proud of my son."

She remained sitting in her pink fuzzy recliner as I walked over and bent down to give her a hug. Her hair smelled a little stale, her perfume from yesterday was just barely still lingering, and I could tell that she had been drinking cold water out of her favorite glass when she kissed me. It doesn't sound like an appetizing combination, but together it was grandma deliciousness. I pulled a little stool close to her recliner because the couch was too far away for us to hold hands, something we always did when it was just the two of us together. Grandma Gladys had moved back to her house in Union City from the nursing home she had been in for a several years. Before that, she had been somewhat of a wanderer. To me, she was always a sweet old lady who spoke gently and would whisper words in my ear that gave me strength and courage, but I knew from looking in her eyes that she was not the typical grandma. My suspicions were confirmed one orated short story at a time through a series of unplanned visits over many years at her many dwellings. In her youth and well into her older age, she was a wild-spirited woman who never cared to cook, moved from town to town often, married seven or eight times, and had at one time developed a taste for Scotch. She was a white woman who had a baby with a black man back in the 70's, an *extremely* brave act of that time period, especially in the southern region of the United States. I never met him, but they produced the most beautiful female I had ever seen- my Aunt Teresa, who we very rarely ever saw. When I was little, I would get her picture from Grandma's jewelry box and carry it around on visits just as this, like an infatuated fan, just so I could look down and gaze at her flawless skin and sparkling eyes. At family gatherings, I was the one who asked where she was and why we hardly ever saw her. The answer was always complicated.

"Well, how are you, sweetheart?" she asked, reaching for my hand, cupping our fingers together in their standard embrace.

"I don't know, Grandma." She could hear the concern in my voice.

"Well, how's that nice handsome boy you're always with?" she asked.

"He's fine, I suppose." She tilted her head and looked at me closer.

"You gonna marry him? You know he wants to," she asked. "They all want to," she said looking at me even closer with a slight grin on her face.

"I don't know, Grandma. He's a really good guy, but there's so much I want to do and see. I know everyone wants me to marry him, but there's something in me that wants something more, but I don't know what it is. You ever felt that way before?" I asked.

She relaxed her shoulders and exhaled out of her nose. "My whole life," she said looking out of the window.

"I don't know what to do. Community Developmental Services asked me to come back and work for them. I could live in one of the group homes like I did my last year of college. Remember? When I lived with those nine mentally handicapped men and took care of them? I could do it again. It would be free rent, and it would be good money. None of my choices seem right when I think about them," I said.

"Did you visit California for that job?" she asked.

"Yes," I said.

"Where did you stay?" she asked.

"The airport," I said.

"No, where did you spend the night?" she asked.

"The International terminal at the airport," I said.

Her eyes got big, "What?"

"I needed to save money, so I just stayed at the airport. The Southwest terminal at LAX isn't open twenty-four hours so I had to stay in the International terminal," I explained.

"They let you?" she asked.

"Yes. I sat in a chair with my suit in the chair next to me. A family from Korea sat near me and I made friends with them. They didn't speak English but we got along great. They brought me soup," I said. "The next morning I got dressed in the airport bathroom and drove to my interview." She looked deep into my eyes and smiled like she was so proud she could almost cry.

"And, how did it go?" she asked.

"Great. They hired me on the spot. It's more pay than I've ever had. They'll even pay me to move out there," I said.

She sat up straight and gasped. "Well, what are you waiting for?"

I looked up at her. I knew she was about to say something big.

"Shoot, you're young! You're healthy! You're beautiful! You're smart! You have a new car! You can go anywhere you want! You have a job waiting for you! You don't have to rely on a man! Go!" she said, looking at me like a football coach calling the last play with five seconds left on the clock.

"But..." I said.

"It can wait. It can all wait, Dalena. Marriage can wait. How many times have you been proposed to?" she asked.

"Six," I said flatly. She laughed.

"Not quite as many as me," she winked.

"It can wait. Marriage can wait. You've stayed near your parents long enough, and you've always been a good daughter. They can wait. This chance... it can't wait. Chances like this don't just happen around every corner. Go for a year and if you don't like it, all you have to do is come back. It's as easy as that," she said. Grandma never ever told me what to do in my personal life. She didn't get involved like that with people. Hearing and seeing her respond like this scared me into taking her more seriously than if this was just another chat. I was stunned. "Tell you what," she said.

"What?" I asked.

"Pray. Pray about it, then you'll know," she said. I hadn't thought to do that. I didn't know if it would even work for something like this, but I was desperate. I needed to make a decision soon. The offer wouldn't last forever. So I took the advice from my grandma which proved to be the best thing that I could do, but only after it proved to be the worst. After I started praying for an answer, I vomited for three days straight. The only time I would stop throwing up is when I thought about moving to California. If I dared think about staying in Tennessee, a feeling of nausea would come crashing down on me like an uncontrollable wave from the angriest ocean. I vomited everywhere: the toilet, the trash can, my front yard, the Walmart parking lot, my dad's garden. I even had to excuse myself from my friend's dinner party to throw up in their backyard. (Sorry, Zoe and Paula.) After three days and a migraine headache, I knew what I had to do. I had to listen to Grandma Gladys. I had to listen to God. I had to find out what the wind was speaking of when I heard its voice in the miracle garden when I was a child. The answer was clear. I had to move to California.

Jalapeño Prawn and Peach Ceviche

Yields: 6-8 servings

"Ceviche" typically means that the seafood protein in the dish is entirely cooked by the process being marinated in the citrus juices. Feel free to do that. I often prefer to cook the prawns until barely pink because I just feel better about it. However, I still call it ceviche.

- 3 peaches or nectarines, peeled, pitted, and diced
- 3 pounds large fresh prawns or shrimp, peeled, deveined, and chopped to size to comfortably fit on your chips
- 1.5 cup finely chopped red onion
- 3/4 cup finely chopped jalapeño, more or less if desired
- Zest of 3 limes
- Juice of 4-5 limes, depending on the juiciness of the limes
- 3/4 tsp. kosher salt
- 3/4 tsp. cayenne pepper (optional)
- 3/4 cup chopped fresh cilantro leaves

- salt and pepper to taste
- olive oil, for cooking the prawns
- Tortilla chips, for serving

Sauté the chopped prawns over medium heat until a slight pink color begins to form. Remove from heat. In a large bowl, combine all other ingredients except cilantro. Add the chopped prawns from the pan. Mix gently and cover with plastic film or lid. Refrigerate for 1 hour. Fold in cilantro leaves, leaving some to garnish on top before serving with tortilla chips.

ASSEMBLY & EATING:

Are you ready for an adventure? Certainly when you eat this you will feel one on its way. It's the marriage of the prawn and peaches together in one place, much like your feet standing on unfamiliar ground but knowing that there is something about the proximity that seems so right. It's the heat of the jalapeño that represents that trials that you will encounter and conquer that will ultimately make you even more tied to the new land. It's the robust red onion representing life's unavoidable but welcomed adventures: loud concerts, pesky neighbors and tiffs with friends. It's the freshness of the cilantro, telling you something new is around the corner. It's the bite, the whole bite, that represents what lies ahead. And away we go.

ACKNOWLEDGMENTS

Camille Phelps, Developmental Editor

Delaney Gray, Editor

Eric Goodman, Esq., Copyright Counsel

Robert Benavente, Esq., Legal Consultant

Aslan Mitchell, Technology Specialist

Devon Benavente, Creative Advisor

Paula Sullivan, Marketing Advisor

Bethany Andrade, Communications Director

Photo Credit

Kenya Mitchell, Director of Photography & Hair Stylist

Camille Phelps, Photographer

OUTsideIN, Wardrobe

Recipe Testers

Rachel O'Donnell, Jackson, TN

Heather Johnson Franks, Murfreesboro, TN

Danilynn Haskins, Lexington, KY

Mariana Ropchan, Orange, CA

Camille Phelps, Southern California

First I'd like to thank God for giving me the vision to write this book and for providing everything that was needed to complete it. Only we know us. I will never bend a knee for another.

I'd like to thank my husband, Rob, and my kids, Aslan and Devon, for the encouragement and love during this process. Y'all are my favorites.

I'd like to thank my mom, dad, sister, and all of my family, along with my friends, teachers and coaches in Northwest Tennessee. You are so special to me.

To my Developmental Editor, Camille Phelps: Thank you for knowing, believing, praying, and for never giving up on me or this book. Your worth is far above rubies. Anyone who disagrees is nothing but a "hater from Decatur who can go eat some tomaters". Thank you, Sis. May God be with you.

To my Editor, Delaney Gray: Any person or organization that has you on their team is blessed beyond measure because excellence is your standard. I handed you scratched down recipes and diary entries housed inside mutilated margins, and you turned them into something this beautiful. Wow, woman. Just, wow. Thank you, dear friend. XOXO

I also want to thank Holly Perry of the *Music City Notes* blog for being a spring board on social media for this book. Your blog is my favorite blog. It's good to be a West Tennessee girl with you. You make me proud.

Made in the USA
Middletown, DE
07 March 2022